MW01625070

THE GROWTH MINDSET COACH

THE GROWTH MINDSET COACH

A Teacher's Month-by-Month Handbook for Empowering Students to Achieve

Annie Brock and Heather Hundley

Published by:
Ulysses Press
P.O. Box 3440
Berkeley, CA 94703
www.ulyssespress.com

Library of Congress Control Number: 2016934493

Printed in the United States
20 19 18 17 16 15 14 13

Acquisitions editor: Casie Vogel
Managing editor: Claire Chun
Editor: Paula Dragosh
Proofreader: Renee Rutledge
Indexer: Jay Kreider
Front cover/interior design and layout: what!design@whatweb.com
Artwork: abstract tree with icons © venimo/shutterstock.com; brain page 41 © Satymova Alena/shutterstock.com; equality/equity illustration page 99 courtesy of Interaction Institute for Social Change | Artist: Angus Maguire

To Abbigail, Addison, Abbott, Bodhi, Lila, and all the children we've met and have yet to meet.

May you face challenges with strength and determination, rise up from failures stronger and wiser than before, and develop a deep, abiding belief in your power to turn wild dreams into great achievements.

CONTENTS

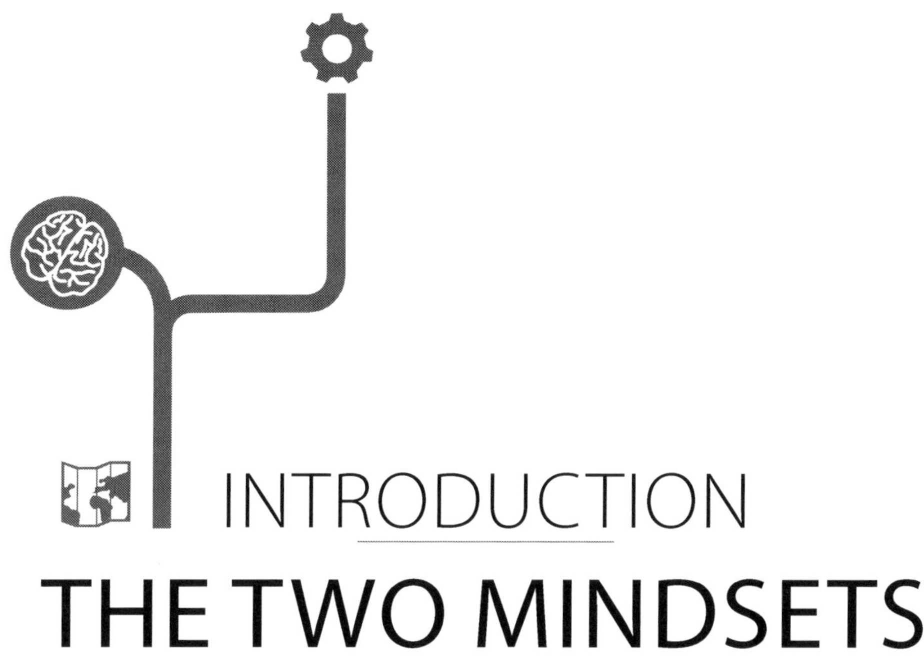

INTRODUCTION
THE TWO MINDSETS

In 2006, Carol Dweck, the Lewis and Virginia Eaton Professor of Psychology at Stanford University, published a book called *Mindset: The New Psychology of Success*. In this chronicle of over thirty years of research into how people succeed, Dweck details her simple, but powerful, theory on two mindsets she discovered in her subjects, which she named the fixed mindset and the growth mindset.[1]

> FIXED MINDSET: The belief that we're born with a fixed amount of intelligence and ability. People operating in the fixed mindset are prone to avoiding challenges and failures, thereby robbing themselves of a life rich in experience and learning.[2]

> GROWTH MINDSET: The belief that with practice, perseverance, and effort, people have limitless potential to learn and grow. People operating in the growth mindset tackle challenges with aplomb, unconcerned with making mistakes or being embarrassed, focusing instead on the process of growth.[3]

These opposing mindsets—fixed and growth—exist in us all, and whether we choose to view various aspects of our lives through the lens of the growth mindset or the fixed mindset can make a big difference. In *Mindset*, Dweck points out that all people begin life with a growth mindset. Indeed, babies are the very picture of the growth mindset. They don't care if what they're saying makes no sense, because they're learning to talk. If they fall down after a few steps, they get right back up, because they're learning to walk.

"What could put an end to this exuberant learning?" asks Dweck in her book. "The fixed mindset. As soon as children become able to evaluate themselves, some of them become afraid of challenges. They become afraid of not being smart."

The Growth Mindset Coach is inspired by Dweck's impressive body of work and research, and offers advice and guidance for teachers who want to tap into the power of the growth mindset. Our experience as classroom teachers has led us to believe wholeheartedly in Dweck's theory that a growth mindset in the classroom can significantly improve student achievement. As teachers we are given opportunities every day to encourage a growth mindset in our students and in members of our school community. In this book, we seek to illuminate specific areas that offer opportunities to cultivate growth mindsets among their students, as well as practical strategies for those who want to seize these opportunities in an effort to empower students to achieve.

HOW TO USE THIS BOOK

Our book is intended to serve as a guide for teachers interested in creating a growth-oriented environment in their classrooms. Transitioning a classroom from the traditional method of instruction and assessment to the growth-mindset way takes a lot of work. We wrote this book to help teachers break down this task into manageable chunks, getting practice in different areas of growth-mindset teaching along the way.

Many of the names and identifying details in this book have been changed to protect the identities of students and colleagues with whom we've worked. Additionally, our teaching experience, while rich and fulfilling, has mostly been practiced in rural, low-income schools, with predominately white and Native American students. The dynamics of our classrooms may be different from classrooms in an urban setting, at a charter school, at a religious school, and so forth. We understand that what has worked for us may not work in every situation, and we encourage you to adapt and modify the resources, tools, and strategies in this book to suit your needs.

Each chapter of *The Growth Mindset Coach* corresponds to a month of the year; each month has a spotlight theme for growth and includes strategies to strengthen your growth-oriented classroom. You'll be engaging with students, parents, and teachers each month to foster the growth mindset in yourself and among classroom and school shareholders. We start by talking through the process of teaching your students about the growth mindset. Once you've learned the basics, you'll spend the year developing your growth mindsets together and taking a deep dive each month into different areas we've identified as central to a growth-oriented classroom. At the end of the year, your students will have had a multifaceted, growth-oriented experience and will be able to use the skills they've learned as they move forward in their educational journey.

Remember, using the growth mindset in teaching is a work in progress. Incorporating a new classroom ethos is a big undertaking! There will be failures, mistakes, and setbacks along the way, but remember to keep a growth mindset about it. Know that each stumbling block is an opportunity to learn something new and improve your methods. It may not be easy, but we guarantee it'll be worth it.

HOW THE BOOK IS ORGANIZED

As we said earlier, each chapter is aligned with a month of the year. If you pick this book up in February, don't sweat it. Just start from the beginning and implement growth-mindset strategies where you can. This isn't an all-or-nothing approach. There's no one right way to create a growth-mindset classroom. Teachers have used a wide variety of tools and strategies to develop and hone their students' growth mindsets. It's not important to us that you follow this book to the letter; it's important that you find what works for you and your students.

Each month begins with a monthly mantra. We're big into repeat-after-me mantras. These are little affirmations that you and your students say together throughout the month to zero in on the monthly goal for growth. In our experience, repeating affirmations helps cement their truth in the minds of your students. Think back to a particularly challenging class you had as a student. If you had started the day by saying "Everyone can learn!" together with your teacher and classmates, would you have felt more confident in your ability to master the course content? We think so! We've watched our own students incorporate class mantras into their regular discourse. One day, you'll overhear a child lean over to a struggling classmate and whisper, "Keep trying. Everyone can learn this," and it'll feel incredible.

In addition to the monthly mantra, each chapter has specific objectives. We provide scientific research, classroom anecdotes, lesson plans, and tips and strategies to help you explore using growth mindset in different areas of teaching.

Let's take a look at what we cover in each chapter:

AUGUST'S MANTRA: Teaching Is a Practice, Not a Perfection

In the first chapter, we talk, in-depth, about the mindsets. You'll familiarize yourself with the definition and characteristics of the two mindsets, and read anecdotes and examples of teaching in the growth and fixed mindsets. We ask you to do some goal setting, reflection, and future thinking so you can start visualizing what your growth-oriented classroom will and will not look like and what effort and adjustments you need to make to get there.

Growth mindset strongly emphasizes process over perfection. You won't have an unassailable growth mindset or a foolproof plan for cultivating growth mindset in others by the end of reading the chapter. We're still working toward those things! But here's a little secret. What's the best way to tell whether you have growth mindset? You still consider yourself a work in progress.

SEPTEMBER'S MANTRA: Everyone Can Learn!

If the central thesis of growth mindset had to be summed up in three words or less it would be "Everyone can learn!" Does this mean that we all have the same potential? No. Does this mean that we're all capable of the same amount of success in any given area? No. Does this mean that if we try hard we'll ace all our schoolwork? No. When we say "Everyone can learn," we simply mean that every person has the potential to develop, grow, and achieve in any given area.

This month you have to do the hard work of convincing your students that no matter where they consider themselves to be in terms of intellect and skill, with hard work and perseverance, they can develop beyond that point. September is all about setting the tone for a growth-oriented year. We provide you with a detailed lesson plan to help teach your students to identify what growth and fixed mindsets are, and convince them that everyone has the ability to achieve.

OCTOBER'S MANTRA: My Brain Is Like a Muscle That Grows!

So you've taught your students the difference between the growth and fixed mindsets, but they're hungry for more information. Like, exactly how is it that our brains learn and grow? This month, we talk about the science behind growth mindset. Neuroplasticity refers to the malleable nature of our brains. You'll dive deep into the world of neurons and dendrites, and give your students a detailed tour of their brains. At the end of the month, they'll understand that, like a muscle, the brain can grow and strengthen with regular practice.

NOVEMBER'S MANTRA: I Am a Valued Member of This Learning Community

This month focuses on relationship building. Tackling challenges and difficult learning tasks with a growth mindset can be scary for students. They wonder, what if I fail? Will I be judged? Will people think that I'm stupid? Students have to believe that their classroom is a safe place in which they can take educational risks. We offer tips and ideas for building stronger relationships with students, parents, and colleagues, because when a strong foundation of meaningful relationships is laid, students are able to show vulnerability and open themselves to new challenges. Only then can they soar to their highest heights.

DECEMBER'S MANTRA: We Love a Challenge!

A student in the growth mindset is motivated to tackle new challenges and overcome obstacles, but if you aren't offering challenging work in the classroom, mindset is largely irrelevant. In this section, we discuss the necessity of sufficiently challenging each student in your class. We also talk about the value of having high expectations for each student. Educational challenges and high expectations are both characteristics of a growth-oriented classroom.

This month, we talk about how to implement a concrete plan for growth and communicate expectations to students and colleagues that sets the tone for the year and serves as a framework for maintaining a growth mindset in the context of learning, because doing hard things is exercise for our brains.

JANUARY'S MANTRA: Feedback Is a Gift—Accept It

Feedback is a critical component of developing a growth-oriented classroom. Much of Dweck's research focuses on praising children in a way that celebrates the effort they put into something, as opposed to their "natural" qualities and talents.

In January, we go in-depth on the concept of person praise (You're so smart) and process praise (You worked really hard on this), and give teachers strategies for incorporating process praise in class. Students should also be equipped with the skills to offer each other appropriate, helpful praise and critique. Teachers who offer feedback only in the form of red check marks or glittery stickers are missing an important opportunity to help students explore steps they can take to improve and make connections between effort and success. Offering specific, timely, purposeful, consistent feedback may have more impact on the growth mindsets of your students than any other practice you engage in this year.

FEBRUARY'S MANTRA: A Goal without a Plan Is Just a Wish

Learning how to set goals and creating a plan for achieving them is important in a growth-oriented classroom. Without the critical component of goal setting, students won't focus on where they want to take their learning. Goal setting is also important to developing the personal characteristic of grit. The idea of grit has gained popularity in educational circles recently.

In February, we look at what grit is, how you can teach your students about grit, and how to help them develop it by helping them pursue goals worthy of their passion and perseverance.

MARCH'S MANTRA: Mistakes Are Opportunities for Learning

In March you'll make efforts to normalize mistakes in the classroom. In the growth mindset, making mistakes and overcoming obstacles in learning are just part of the path to mastery. But all too often, the fear of making mistakes keeps students from taking on challenges. We share with you ways to reframe student mistakes as valuable learning opportunities, as well as offer ideas for coaching students through setbacks. Learning shouldn't be neat; learning is messy and full of peaks and pitfalls and two steps forward and one step back. In the growth mindset, you don't just anticipate mistakes, you embrace them as an integral part of the learning process. We also discuss strategies for creating opportunities for "productive struggle" in your classroom.

APRIL'S MANTRA: There's a Difference Between Not Knowing and Not Knowing Yet!

Yet is a tiny word with a big meaning. This month, you'll learn how the power of yet can reinforce growth mindset in learning. You'll even meet some teachers who are replacing grades with "not yets." April is all about helping you formulate a plan to incorporate the power of yet in your classroom through purposeful formative and summative assessment, as well as offering twists on evaluation that emphasize mastery over letter grades. And we share ways that you can empower students to direct their own learning, provide opportunities for them to think critically to solve authentic problems, and help them practice essential skills relevant to the real world.

MAY'S MANTRA: I Got This!

May has arrived, and it's time to send your students home for the summer. But how can you make sure their growth-mindset training doesn't get lost on the summer slide? This chapter is about equipping students with the tools they'll need to continue using growth mindset in their educational and personal lives after they leave your classroom. We teach you the value of self-talk and coach you through helping students develop a plan to control the fixed-mindset voice that lives in their head. Finally, you'll help students establish a plan for using growth mindset over the summer to reinforce your mindset instruction.

JUNE'S MANTRA: I Can't Take Care of Others If I Don't Take Care of Myself

June is all about reflection, relaxation, and renewal. We walk you through guided journaling with questions and prompts to help you engage in deep reflection about your growth-mindset experience. We also talk about the value of sharpening the saw—or taking care of your personal needs—during the summer months as a way to develop healthy habits and renew your mind, body, and spirit after a year of hard work.

JULY'S MANTRA: A New Day Is a New Opportunity to Grow

Summertime is your chance to shift out of teaching mode and fully engage your learning mode. This month is packed full of growth-mindset resources you can use to further your training, as well as tips and strategies for practicing growth mindset in everyday situations. We also give you advice for developing an online personal learning network through Twitter and other social media platforms in order to extend your base of support and deepen your well of knowledge.

The Growth Mindset Coach is a guidebook on your journey to developing your growth mindset and fostering the growth mindsets of your students. It's important to acknowledge that this is a journey that has no end. As Dweck writes, "The path to growth mindset is a journey, not a proclamation." In other words, if someone definitively declares "I have a growth mindset," that person is lying to you. Mindset is not an either-or thing. We all have a fixed mindset *and* a growth mindset; it's just a matter of deciding which one to use in any given situation. Even if you become highly attuned to your growth mindset, you can rest assured that your fixed mindset will remain firmly in your head, waiting to beckon to you to join it in avoiding a challenge or wallowing in failure. Through the process described in this chapter, we hope to teach you how to engage your growth mindset and curb your fixed mindset, fortify yourself with the necessary skills and strategies to live a life devoted to learning and growing, and use our tools to foster growth mindset in your students.

1

AUGUST: TEACHING IS A PRACTICE, NOT A PERFECTION

It does not matter how slowly you go, so long as you do not stop.

— Confucius

OBJECTIVES

- ✓ Familiarize yourself with growth and fixed mindsets.
- ✓ Reflect on the mindsets of your former teachers.
- ✓ Set goals to incorporate growth mindset in the upcoming school year.

MINDSETS

For many years, people have bought into the notion that certain abilities and qualities of our nature are fixed. You might have heard someone say "I'm not athletic" or "I'm not a math person," or you might've even said something like this yourself. And up until recently, many of us have accepted that there are certain unchangeable aspects of ourselves. Archetypal media representations of nerds, jocks, and meatheads have furthered the notion that certain people are simply destined for certain outcomes that are off-limits to others. That is, until Carol Dweck's *Mindset* was published and read by millions the world over.

In *Mindset,* Dweck lays out the evidence she and her team collected through years of research, which reinforces a simple, but powerful, theory: human intelligence, creativity, athleticism, and other qualities are not fixed traits that we're born with. Rather, they're malleable ones that with time and effort can be changed.[4] Dweck identifies two types of what she calls "mindsets" in her research: growth and fixed.

FIXED MINDSET: Assumes that intelligence and other qualities, abilities, and talents are fixed traits that cannot be significantly developed.

Those with a fixed mindset have bought into the idea, often from a very early age, that things like intelligence and other talents and abilities are of a fixed nature — they cannot be changed. A fixed mindset believes people have a certain amount of talent and intelligence in any given area. In other words, if you aren't naturally gifted at something or don't catch on to it right away, you might as well forget it. Often people of the fixed mindset work very hard to shed light on those areas in which they "naturally" excel and cover up areas in which they don't.

GROWTH MINDSET: Assumes that intelligence and other qualities, abilities, and talents can be developed with effort, learning, and dedication.

People with a growth mindset view themselves in an altogether different way than those with a fixed mindset. A person who tends toward the growth mindset sees things like intelligence or artistic and athletic abilities not as fixed traits but as qualities that can be changed and improved with time and effort. A growth mindset operates under the assumption that our qualities are not inherent or natural or that we're only given so much of them, but that our willingness to learn, our effort, and our persistence dictate how adept we become at any given pursuit.

The growth mindset does not buy into the idea that there are "math people" or "creative people" or "athletic people," but with hard work and perseverance, anyone can achieve success in any area.

Once a person learns to harness the growth mindset, the powerful forces of growth take over. No longer are failures viewed through a lens of disappointment and shame, but through one of opportunity for improvement. The growth mindset doesn't ignore the fact that some of us may have more inherent aptitude for some things—we've all seen children with a seemingly natural affinity for singing beautifully, hitting home runs, or reading beyond their years—rather, it understands that aptitude can be fortified with experience and effort, bolstered with resilience, and ultimately lead to great success regardless of the starting point. Does that mean we're all just a few singing lessons away from becoming the next Adele? Not in the least. It just means, as Dweck says, "that a person's true potential is unknown (and unknowable); that it's impossible to foresee what can be accomplished with years of passion, toil, and training."[5]

EXAMPLES OF GROWTH MINDSET

History is filled with paragons of growth mindset—people who have worked hard, refused to give up, and succeeded against all odds. American history is rich with stories of people like the pioneers, who battled brutal conditions as they headed West toward the promise of a better life, or the activists of the civil rights movement, who stood up against the systemic oppression they endured long after slavery ended and worked tirelessly for change at great personal risk.

Growth mindset can be seen in individual stories, as well—groundbreaking people who worked hard to turn dreams into realities.

The Olympic track star Wilma Rudolph started life as a premature baby in 1940s-era Tennessee, the twentieth of her father's twenty-two children. After battling scarlet fever and polio, she lost the use of her leg at just six years old. Her mother took her to weekly treatments, and her siblings massaged her leg every day. By the time she was nine, Rudolph had shed her leg brace and started moving. Later, her legs would carry her to gold in the 1960 Rome Olympics.[6]

Remember the movie *Rudy*? It's based on the story of Rudy Ruettiger, a working-class kid from Joliet, Illinois, whose childhood dream was to attend the University of Notre Dame. Despite a challenging dyslexia diagnosis and three rejections from Notre Dame, Rudy eventually was admitted to the prestigious university, where he set his sights on joining the football team. Through his displays of indefatigable work ethic, the five-foot-six-inch Rudy made it on the scout squad, and later into a single game, where in the final three plays he made one of the most memorable quarterback sacks in college football history.[7]

Supreme Court Justice Sonia Sotomayor grew up in the impoverished projects of the Bronx. Her mother began life as an orphan in Puerto Rico, and her father had only a third-grade education. Her mother emphasized the value of work ethic and education as a path to success, and young Sonia worked tirelessly at her studies, despite dealing with the effects of her father's alcoholism and early death, and her own diabetic condition, eventually earning a spot in the Ivy League. Sotomayor gives much of the credit for her success to those who helped her along the way, though it's clear her hard work and willingness to confront any challenge or obstacle contributed significantly to her incredible journey.[8]

Marie Curie is another exemplar of the growth mindset. Born in war-torn, politically charged Warsaw, Poland, where women, particularly Polish women, were not allowed to pursue higher education, Curie had to create opportunities, often at great personal risk, to learn about math, chemistry, and physics—the subjects she loved. Later she became the first woman to win a Nobel Prize.[9]

Malala Yousafzai was a ten-year-old girl from Pakistan with a zeal for education when Taliban forces infiltrated her region and banned girls from attending school. Malala's unwavering belief in her right to an education led her to start an anonymous blog, where she wrote about her desire to go to school and quickly became a voice for disenfranchised Pakistani girls being robbed of an education. When she was fifteen years old, Malala was riding a bus home when it was stopped by Taliban forces; one fighter boarded the bus, asked for Malala by name, and then shot her in the head. Against all odds, Malala survived the attack and refused to let the bullet silence her, redoubling her efforts to fight for equal rights in education. In 2014 Malala Yousafzai became the youngest-ever winner of the Nobel Peace Prize, and to this day she continues to advocate on behalf of girls all over the world in need of quality education.[10]

People who cultivate a growth mindset are more resilient in the face of setbacks or obstacles. The growth mindset, after all, relishes the process of learning, not achievement. While someone of a fixed mindset revels in success and admiration for being able to learn and accomplish with seemingly little to no effort, a person in the growth mindset is not satisfied with superficial achievement. When failure comes to people with a fixed mindset, as it inevitably does, they're far less equipped to deal with it because, in their mind, it speaks to their inadequacy as a person, rather than a challenge to be overcome or an obstacle to be negotiated. When failure comes to people with the growth mindset, on the other hand, they view it as a learning opportunity that will serve them as they try again.

Whether a person operates in the growth or fixed mindset may seem like a small thing, but consider that mindset is present in virtually every aspect of our lives. From decision making to career goals to romantic relationships to parenting, our mindsets heavily influence the lens through which we see the world. And, ultimately, our mindset affects those around us.

YOUR DAILY MINDSET

In *Mindset,* Carol Dweck tells readers that as they learn more about the two mindsets, they will begin to see "how a belief that your qualities are carved in stone leads to a host of thoughts and actions, and how a belief that your qualities can be cultivated leads to a host of different thoughts and actions."[11] The narrative Dweck has constructed around the mindsets based on her research and observation shows, without a doubt, people operating in the growth mindset experience different, arguably better, outcomes than those who operate in the fixed mindset.

Consider your own mindset for a moment. Do you exhibit the characteristics of a growth or fixed mindset? Most likely, you display a bit of both. Growth and fixed mindsets are dichotomous ideas that exist on a spectrum, and even though you may have designs on becoming a fully realized exemplar of growth mindset, you'll likely always be on your journey toward that ideal. We must recognize and accept that we're all a mixture of the two mindsets — growth and fixed — and, although it may become more intuitive with practice, we'll always have to be intentional about employing our growth mindset. It may appear that we're presenting growth and fixed mindsets as a sort of mindset binary, but mindset isn't an either-or proposition. All people have both mindsets; it's more a matter of which mindset you're prone to defaulting to in certain situations. For example, a person could have a growth mindset about learning new languages, but a fixed mindset about losing weight. Even Dweck, the growth mindset expert, calls herself out in her own book for falling into the fixed-mindset trap from time to time.[12]

Before we discuss how to bring the growth mindset to your classroom, it's important to understand where you fall on the mindset spectrum. Below we've listed a series of statements. Check all the statements with which you agree.

1. ____ There are just some things I'll never be good at.
2. ____ When I make a mistake, I try to learn from it.
3. ____ When others do better than me, I feel threatened.
4. ____ I enjoy getting out of my comfort zone.
5. ____ When I show others I'm smart or talented, I feel successful.
6. ____ I feel inspired by the success of others.
7. ____ I feel good when I can do something others cannot.
8. ____ It's possible to change how intelligent you are.
9. ____ You shouldn't have to try to be smart—you just are or you aren't.
10. ____ I enjoy taking on a new challenge or task with which I am unfamiliar.

In this assessment, the odd-numbered statements (1, 3, 5, 7, 9) indicate a fixed mindset, while the even-numbered statements (2, 4, 6, 8, 10) illustrate a growth mindset. It's important to know where you are as a starting point, but whether you're more closely aligned with a fixed or a growth mindset or a mixture of the two, the goal of this book is the same—to hone your growth mindset and put it to work in your classroom. And, as we know from years of growth-mindset research, your ability to grow and change in this regard depends on the amount of work you're willing to do.

Dweck identified five key areas in which the actions of people of opposing mindsets often diverge: challenges, obstacles, effort, criticism, and success of others.[13] In the fixed mindset, a response to any of the five situations typically relates to the person's desire to look smart and avoid failure; in the growth mindset the response more likely stems from the person's desire to learn and improve. Let's look at both fixed- and growth-mindset responses to each of these five situations.

SITUATION	FIXED MINDSET	GROWTH MINDSET
CHALLENGES	Challenges are avoided to maintain the appearance of intelligence.	Challenges are embraced, stemming from a desire to learn.
OBSTACLES	Giving up in the face of obstacles and setbacks is a common response.	Showing perseverance in the face of obstacles and setbacks is a common response.
EFFORT	Having to try or put in effort is viewed as a negative; if you have to try, you're not very smart or talented.	Doing hard work and putting in effort paves the path to achievement and success.
CRITICISM	Negative feedback, regardless of how constructive, is ignored.	Criticism provides important feedback that can aid in learning.
SUCCESS OF OTHERS	Other people's success is viewed as a threat and evokes feelings of insecurity or vulnerability.	Other people's success can be a source of inspiration and education.

GROWTH MINDSET AT SCHOOL

Now that you understand what growth mindset is, you're probably wondering what the science of mindset means for teachers. Teachers who strive to develop a growth mindset are a lot different from teachers who operate under the fixed mindset. Let's take a look at what the self-talk of a fixed-mindset teacher might look like in comparison to that of a growth-mindset teacher.

FIXED MINDSET	GROWTH MINDSET
Professional development is so boring; I never learn anything at these things.	During professional development, I'll listen with an open mind and seek out new ideas.
This parent is driving me crazy; he wants a progress update every day.	This parent is very invested; I need to find a way to communicate with him productively.
This student is incapable of making gains in math.	How can I present the information so this student will understand?
This student is a brilliant reader; she doesn't need my attention.	I should develop enrichment opportunities so this student feels sufficiently challenged in reading instruction.
I'll never be as good a teacher as she is.	I should ask her to be my mentor so I can learn from her.
My students ruined this lesson; they just refused to cooperate.	How could I change this lesson so it's more engaging for my students?
This student hates school, and there's nothing I can do to change that.	How can I use this student's interests and passions to engage her in learning?
With his poor home life, this student doesn't have a prayer of graduating.	I believe that this student can find success, regardless of his background.

Do you see the difference? The fixed-mindset teacher approaches situations as unchangeable. A bad lesson plan is a total failure never to be revisited. A needy parent will always be a source of annoyance. Professional development is a total waste of time. But a growth-mindset teacher approaches these same situations with a completely different point of view. A bad lesson plan is a trial run that went off course and can be tweaked to work better next time. A needy parent isn't needy; he or she is invested, and it's just a matter of figuring out how best to communicate. And professional development is a chance to learn something new, talk to colleagues, and spend some much-needed time thinking about the mechanics of teaching.

Oftentimes, using your growth mindset simply means a change in self-talk. Instead of writing someone off, you seek to find ways to make learning more accessible for that person. Instead of throwing in the towel, you figure out another way to attack the problem. Instead of letting jealousy or feelings of inadequacy take center stage, you focus on how you can improve.

As you work through the subsequent chapters, you'll discover our purpose in writing this book is twofold. First, we want to help you, the teacher, look inward and find and hone the voice of growth mindset in your head. The fact is, we all have fixed and growth mindsets. Perhaps your natural inclination is in the fixed mindset, and that's okay. The trick is to respond to your inner fixed voice with your inner growth voice in order to reframe challenges and setbacks as opportunities for growth instead of personal failures. Second, we want you to take that inner voice of growth and unleash it in your school. We walk through strategies for using the growth mindset to help your students, colleagues, and parents embrace challenge, failure, and mistakes, not fear them. We want you and others to see that with patience, effort, and time, it's possible to achieve success in any realm of study.

The growth-mindset teacher has the ability to positively influence student performance, in addition to getting more from relationships and fostering a growth-oriented school culture. In this book, we examine how a teacher can use the principle of the growth mindset to change his or her classroom, school, and community for the better. We believe that your mindset changes the way you relate to the people around you, and that mindset is infectious. The research shows that when you can get students to buy into the idea that the brain, like a muscle, has the capacity to strengthen and grow, the result is better motivation, stronger resolve to succeed, and higher academic achievement.[14]

CAN GROWTH MINDSET FIX OUR SCHOOLS?

Is adopting the growth mindset a cure-all for what ails America's school system? Certainly not. We know, for example, that an achievement gap exists that is strongly correlated with poverty and race — a systemic problem that cannot be solved by simply telling students to work harder and persevere. We aren't suggesting that teachers and schools use the growth mindset to the exclusion of other solutions for the discrepancies in and barriers to achievement. As Dweck wrote in *Education Week*, "The growth mindset was intended to help close achievement gaps, not hide them. It's about telling the truth about a student's current achievement, and then, together, doing something about it, helping him or her become smarter."[15]

Our position is that growth mindset should be practiced in connection with strong pedagogy and robust curriculum, not instead of it. It's important that kids put in effort and believe that they can achieve success in their schoolwork, but we as teachers must offer up learning experiences that are engaging, valuable, accessible, and meaningful in order for growth mindset to make a true difference in learning outcomes. Growth mindset is a way of thinking that allows for individuals to put aside fear of failure or looking stupid, and focus on learning—which is something students from all backgrounds wrestle with.

Can you imagine how limiting school must feel for students who believe there's a cap on their intelligence? The moment they encounter struggle, it's a big red flag telling them they might as well give up. Teaching your students about the power of the growth mindset means removing the false limitations they've put on themselves, and opening them up to possibilities previously thought out of reach because of distorted assumptions about their own intelligence, talent, and skills. Of course, only you can control your own mindset. It's the inner monologue that so often is the difference between approaching a challenge with the growth mindset over the fixed. You may not be able to personally change the fixed mindset of the teacher down the hall, or the student who insists she's not a "math person," or the parent who has a mistrust of education rooted in his or her own negative experience, but you can teach, model, and coach the growth mindset in a way that inspires others to see their own potential for success.

YOUR BEST/WORST TEACHERS

In discussing the idea for this book, we asked people about their negative and positive school experiences, and we quickly realized that, even though it didn't have a name at the time, most people's worst experiences revolved around interactions with educators who had a fixed mindset, and some of the best experiences were made possible by growth-oriented teachers.

One person remembered being victimized by a middle school teacher who organized the classroom seating chart from best test performance to worst, and the subsequent anxiety triggered by the possibility of winding up in the front row with the kids who had been very publicly declared stupid by this misguided educator. This was not a teacher interested in turning failures into opportunities to do better, but one who reinforced the wrongheaded idea that it's more important to appear smart in front of one's peers than to authentically engage in the practice of learning regardless of your starting point.

Another person recalled a discussion about college with a school counselor, who pointed out, upon review of the student's grades, that she was obviously not a "math and science person" and should focus on her writing talents. Whether the student would have naturally gravitated toward writing as a career path remains unknown, but she said that as a seventeen-year-old kid she just accepted, at the word of this educator, that anything in the math and science field was off the table for her because it just "wasn't my thing." She later discovered a strong interest in math and science, when she realized that she not only had the capacity to understand math and science as learning disciplines, but really enjoyed them, as well.

Many others we approached had similar stories of how the fixed-mindset attitude of an educator had a negative impact on the course of their lives. As plentiful as the stories are of the fixed mindset wreaking havoc on the confidence and perseverance of young people, so too are the stories of growth-oriented teachers encouraging students to stick with something and overcome challenges in the learning process. In fact, you'll often find these qualities recounted when people discuss their favorite teachers. Think back to your favorite teacher for a moment. Why was he or she a favorite?

Three reasons why ______________________________ was my favorite teacher:

1. ______________________________

____

2. ______________________________

____

3. ______________________________

____

Now think back to an ineffective or unlikable teacher. Why was he or she ineffective or unlikable?

Three reasons why ______________________ was my least effective teacher:

1. ____

____

2. ____

____

3. ____

____

Do any of the items you listed fall into the growth- or fixed-mindset categories? Consider whether your best loved and least liked or most and least effective teachers had a growth or fixed mindset, and how those mindsets affected you as a learner.

TEACH, a United States Department of Education initiative and coalition between public, private, and governmental organizations to support teaching and American education, interviewed several successful people about their favorite teachers. Let's see if your answers about why your favorite teacher is so memorable are similar to their descriptions of favorite teachers.

- Arne Duncan, former US secretary of education, describes his favorite high school English teacher like this: "She worked us hard. She challenged us. It wasn't easy work. There was never talk about limits or ceilings or what you can't do. She was always pushing you. As good as you thought you were, she was pushing you to the next level."[16]
- Chris Paul, an NBA superstar, said, "Ms. Felder was my 10th grade biology teacher. She may be somewhere saying I'm just okay in the NBA, but if I would have stuck to it, I could have been a biology teacher. When you have good

people to tell you that when you work hard, anything is possible, you can have a lasting imprint on someone's life."[17]

- Steven Chu, former US secretary of energy, describes how his favorite teacher valued learning over right answers. "He wasn't trying to teach us facts. He was actually trying to teach us a learning process. Learning whether you understand something or not was the most important thing I began to learn in his class. That lesson I took with me not only through college and graduate school, but through my entire career as a physicist."[18]
- "He used to say the greatest gift a teacher or parent can ever give a kid is confidence," said Julia Louis-Dreyfus, an Emmy-award winning actress, of her high school physics teacher Mr. Coyne. "He even allowed the experiments we did to be funny. As a result, I don't find science scary or daunting. I love science."[19]

Are you sensing a theme? When people remember their favorite teachers, it typically isn't the teachers who let them breeze by or show off how great they were. It's not the teachers who made them feel certain subjects or pursuits were off-limits because they weren't naturally gifted at them. Rather, the most memorable and influential teachers were the ones who pushed and challenged their students. These teachers made learning accessible and valued and emphasized the process of learning, not just the outcomes.

This is what the growth mindset is all about: practice and persistence as a path to achievement, getting outside a comfort zone to take on new challenges, and recognizing that setbacks and failures are just part of the process.

PREP FOR YOUR YEAR OF GROWTH MINDSET

Now that you've familiarized yourself with the fixed and growth mindsets, and looked on your history as a learner to consider the characteristics of fixed- and growth-mindset teachers in your own life, it's time to prepare an action plan to get your year of growth underway. Let's start by writing a SMART goal related to developing your growth mindset and fostering it in others. Use the same formula to write a few more.

There will be times when teaching with a growth mindset will prove frustrating. It'll take endless amounts of patience and resolve to encourage students to try a new strategy when they've given up. It'll take changing the way you offer praise and feedback. It'll take intentional, purposeful interactions with everyone you meet. And it'll be worth it.

MY GROWTH-MINDSET SMART GOAL

Specific—Write a specific description of your growth-mindset goal

Measurable—Write how you plan to track progress toward the goal

Actionable—Write specific steps you can take toward attaining your goal

Realistic—Write what resources and supports you need to achieve the goal

Timely—Write your deadline for achieving your goal

Here is an example of what a SMART goal related to growth mindset might look like:

- By the second week of school, I will be able to call my students by name and know one of their personal interests outside school. To achieve my goal, I will make a point to use student names as often as possible and have students fill out an interest inventory. I will keep track of this information on my photo seating chart, and test myself on my progress weekly.

This goal is specific to building relationships with students. Progress can easily be measured by self-testing knowledge of each student's name and interest. The action items here include using the students' names as often as possible in conversation and asking them to fill out an interest inventory. Other action steps that would be appropriate to this goal might be greeting students by name at the door each morning, having students participate in icebreaker games to reveal their interests, or creating an "All About Me" interactive bulletin board with photos and facts about each student. This goal is realistic in nature, because two weeks is a reasonable amount of time in which to learn student names. A library media specialist, who works with all the students in the school, might need a bit more time. Just make sure that your goal is realistic! The goal is timely because your deadline isn't too far off and provides an adequate amount of time to learn the new information.

Now, you try! First, break down the components of your SMART goal.

S ______________________________

M ______________________________

A ______________________________

R ______________________________

T ______________________________

Using the components above, write your growth-mindset goal below.

____

____

____

____

____

____

____

____

____

____

____

____

____

____

2

SEPTEMBER: EVERYONE CAN LEARN!

No matter what your ability is, effort is what ignites that ability and turns it into accomplishment.

— Carol Dweck, *Mindset*

OBJECTIVES

- ✓ Teach your students about the mindsets.
- ✓ Establish your classroom as a growth-mindset zone.
- ✓ Create a climate of growth mindset with parents and students.

When Ashley entered kindergarten, her teacher knew right away she was dealing with a case of fixed mindset. Whenever Ashley met a challenge that might give her the slightest bit of difficulty, she'd cross her arms, cry, and stomp away.

"I'm never coming back to school!" she would proclaim, after encountering a bit of difficulty in completing a task. "I can't get this. It's too hard."

Ashley's teacher began a rigorous growth-mindset intervention. Whenever Ashley gave up after only the slightest bit of effort, her teacher encouraged her to try again. When Ashley tried again, the teacher praised her for putting in effort. One day, Ashley's teacher told her about the fixed and growth mindsets. She told Ashley that having a positive attitude toward learning included taking on challenges and learning from mistakes. She told Ashley to never feel bad about making a mistake, because making mistakes is how the brain learns and grows. Every time Ashley made a mistake or got frustrated, her teacher would say, "Oh, look! Your brain is growing!"

Little by little, Ashley became more confident in her learning. She'd try new things, attempt to make new friends, and tackle other learning and social challenges in ways she hadn't been willing to before. Ashley's teacher had shown her the power of the growth mindset. By the end of the year, the disinterested and defensive girl had transformed into an engaged, curious learner confident in her ability to conquer difficult tasks.

Research has shown that teaching students the concept of growth mindset can have positive implications on student achievement, like it did with Ashley. In fact, researchers have begun to see results with as little as one forty-five-minute lesson on brain development and the mindsets.[20]

RESEARCH ON THE VALUE OF TEACHING GROWTH MINDSET

The Project for Education Research That Scales (PERTS), an applied research center at Stanford University, is dedicated to researching academic motivation and counts Carol Dweck and mindset rock stars David Yeager and Jo Boaler (author of *Mathematical Mindsets*, a must-read for teachers interested in using growth mindset in math instruction) among its research collaborators. Much of the work done at PERTS focuses on the mindsets. David Paunesku, executive director of PERTS, along with his colleagues, published a paper in 2015 on mindset training as a viable way to increase student motivation and achievement.

Paunesku and his colleagues wanted to devise a way to improve academic achievement that can work not just in one specific school but be scaled to schools across the nation. The researchers tested two types of psychological interventions meant to improve student achievement.[21] The first was referred to as a "sense of purpose" intervention, which helped students understand how their education would help them achieve their long-term goals. Basically, it answered the why questions students often have: Why should I learn? Why does this work matter? The second type of intervention was a mindset intervention, in which students learned about the growth mindset, specifically that all people are capable of learning, and that struggle and challenge in academic work is simply part of the learning process and not an indication of failure or inadequacy.

Of the students who participated in the interventions, about a third were labeled at risk for becoming high school dropouts. Looking at the scores of these at-risk students, the researchers found a noticeable increase in the grade point averages of the students receiving the interventions.

Other research also indicates a strong correlation between mindset training and improved grades and engagement. One found that students who received training in the mindsets showed improved test scores, and girls who received the training outperformed girls who did not receive it in math, which suggests a potential strategy for closing the long-established gender gap in math education.[22]

Another study found that students who learned the growth mindset showed increases in academic achievement, and it also noted a specific increase for African American students, who reported attitudes of valuing and enjoying school more after the mindset training, which shows potential as a strategy for narrowing the racial achievement gap.[23]

So what's this body of research telling us? Students learning about growth mindset are learning that they're capable of achievement in all areas and then going on to prove it. They're receiving the message that the brain is capable of growth, but must be pushed and exercised to experience that growth. Once students get the message, they're able to apply it to the work they're doing in school. In other words, when students are taught that everyone is capable of achieving in all areas, they achieve at higher rates.

This subtle shift in perspective makes a big difference, and it made us wonder: if students showed improvement with just a single forty-five-minute intervention, how might they change when exposed to a sustained growth-mindset program for a year?

An important part of adopting the growth mindset in your classroom is to teach students exactly what constitutes a growth mindset and how they can harness its power. We know educating students about healthy eating and nutrition early on can help them avoid obesity and its associated health problems in the future. We know comprehensive sex education is associated with a lower risk for teen pregnancy. But when it comes to understanding how our bodies learn and how our brains are motivated to achieve, we don't really discuss it. Isn't it interesting that the one thing students and teachers are meant to do every day—dedicate themselves to the process of learning and growth—is the one process we never really bother talking about? Well, we think it's time for a change, and we're not the only ones.

After research findings indicated a positive association with growth mindset intervention and student achievement, PERTS developed Mindset Kit (www.mindsetkit.org), which is an excellent starting point for educators interested in teaching growth mindset to their students. There are free online lesson plans, activities, and videos that teachers can access. PERTS has also partnered with Khan Academy, a renowned personalized learning organization with thousands of instructional videos and lessons across a broad range of subjects, to create a growth mindset lesson plan. There's also a resource library where teachers can post and share materials for teaching growth mindset. These are all excellent places to access materials for teaching growth mindset, and we encourage you to explore them. At the end of this chapter we also share a list of helpful mindset resources.

Using *Mindset* and the Mindset Kit online as inspiration, we've developed our own growth-mindset lesson plan. Remember our mantra for the month? Everyone can learn! We don't just want your kids to say it, we want them to believe it! Your students, many of whom may already be deeply rooted in the fixed mindset like Ashley, aren't going to blindly accept the idea that everyone can learn without a little bit of convincing. So we've put together this lesson plan to guide you as you embark on your journey to create a growth-oriented classroom. The simplicity of the growth mindset is such that students from kindergarten through college can easily understand what it is and how to practice it, but there's no one-size-fits-all way to teach growth mindset. Consider your school culture, students, and classroom dynamics, and then adapt and differentiate this plan to make it work for you and your students.

THE GROWTH MINDSET

LESSON PLAN

LEARNING OBJECTIVES

By the end of this lesson, students will be able to:

- explain the difference between growth and fixed mindsets.
- distinguish between examples of growth and fixed mindsets.
- understand everyone is born to learn and we're all at a different place in our learning.

SETTING UP THE LESSON

Cultivating a climate for learning and fostering the growth mindset are essential to empowering students to achieve. Researchers and educators have developed many ways to help students embrace a growth mindset. Here are a few ideas to help you explicitly teach your students about growth and fixed mindsets, ways to help students identify the mindsets, and activities related to learning and growing the brain.

RESOURCES AND MATERIALS

- Computer and video projection capabilities
- Access to YouTube
- Marker board or large writing surface for brainstorming and web building
- Graphic organizers, including T-charts and foldables
- Markers/crayons/pencils

ESSENTIAL QUESTIONS

How do we learn new things?

Why is having a growth mindset valuable to learning?

How does understanding fixed and growth mindset help us meet our goals?

PART 1: EVERYONE CAN LEARN!

STEP 1: Preflection

Before viewing the video, ask the students to ***think, draw, or write*** about the following questions:

- Think of a time you learned something new. What steps did you take to learn it?
- Think of a time you failed at something. How did it make you feel? What happened after you failed?

Optional Ideas for Extension Activity: If you want to further explore the feelings that success and failure can evoke in your students, consider doing an extension activity. Students can create a comic strip with four simple pictures, write a poem or song, or create a short video to detail the learning process as they have experienced it.

STEP 2: Video and Discussion

Watch the video "You Can Learn Anything" (0:90), published by Khan Academy. It points out that Shakespeare, at some point, had to learn his ABCs, and there was a time Einstein couldn't count to ten. Have the students write an example of something someone acclaimed in their field would have had to learn before they were successful. For example, Serena Williams had to learn how to hit a tennis ball; Mark Zuckerberg had to learn how to type. Ask students to volunteer to share ideas they have generated.

STEP 3: Student Reflection

Older students can work in small groups to generate a T-chart of things they have learned and a prerequisite skill they needed in order to learn it.

Younger students can use a four-section foldable to draw pictures of something they've learned to do. Under each flap, have students illustrate something they had to learn first. For example, on the outside they may have drawn a soccer ball, so on the inside they would draw walking or running as a prerequisite skill for playing soccer.

Name: ______________________________

I have learned to . . .

SAMPLE DRAWING: T-Chart

I LEARNED THIS.	BUT FIRST I NEEDED TO KNOW THIS.

SAMPLE DRAWING: Foldable

STEP 4: Essential Question Connection

These activities lend themselves to answering our first essential question: How do we learn new things? We learn by building one skill on top of another, persevering through mistakes, and growing our brain.

STEP 5: Explain

Tell students about a time that you had to struggle to learn something. Describe in detail what you had to do to overcome the challenge, making sure to touch on the following areas:

- The effort you had to put in.
- Problem-solving strategies you used.
- How you sought help from others.

STEP 6: Activity: Think, Pair, Share

Allow students to share their experiences with a partner.

Encourage them to **Think** of a time they had difficulty learning something, **Pair** up with a partner, and **Share** with each other the experience, what they learned, and the outcome. Each student gets one minute to share. Allow students to meet with several classmates to discuss their experiences.

End of Part I. Combine Part I and Part II of lesson, or continue to Part II next class period.

PART 2: GROWTH AND FIXED MINDSETS

STEP 1: Self-Assessment

Students self-assess their mindsets using the following mindset quiz.

Directions: Read each statement and decide if it is **TRUE** or **FALSE** for you. Circle your answer.

1. If I have to work hard at something, it means that I'm not smart.
   TRUE or **FALSE**
2. I like to try things that are hard.
   TRUE or **FALSE**
3. When I make a mistake, I get embarrassed.
   TRUE or **FALSE**
4. I like to be told I'm smart.
   TRUE or **FALSE**
5. I usually quit when something gets difficult or frustrating.
   TRUE or **FALSE**
6. I don't mind making mistakes. They help me learn.
   TRUE or **FALSE**
7. There are some things I'll never be good at.
   TRUE or **FALSE**
8. Anyone can learn something if they work hard at it.
   TRUE or **FALSE**
9. People are born stupid, average, or smart, and can't change it.
   TRUE or **FALSE**
10. Doing my best makes me proud, even if it's not perfect.
    TRUE or **FALSE**

How many of the odd-numbered statements did you think were true?

____

How many of the even-numbered statements did you think were true?

____

Evaluating the Assessment: Odd-numbered statements are characteristic of a fixed mindset; even-numbered statements are characteristic of a growth mindset. Ask students if, based on the results, they have a fixed mindset, a growth mindset, or a mixture of the two.

Extension Activity: Have students give themselves one point for marking TRUE on an odd-numbered statement and one point for marking FALSE on an even-numbered statement. Ten points indicate a strong fixed mindset; zero points indicate a strong growth mindset. Plot the results to use later as a visual for explaining how most people are a mixture of the two mindsets.

STEP 2: Explore Mindsets

Present fixed- and growth-mindset definitions:

FIXED MINDSET: Assumes intelligence and other qualities, abilities, and talents are fixed traits that cannot be significantly developed.

GROWTH MINDSET: Assumes intelligence and other qualities, abilities, and talents can be developed with effort, learning, and dedication over time.

Post these definitions prominently in the classroom so students can reference them easily.

Review the results of student self-assessments. Tell students that everyone possesses both fixed and growth mindsets, and this year they'll be learning strategies to promote their growth mindsets. But first, they'll learn more about fixed and growth mindsets so they can easily recognize them and distinguish between the two.

STEP 3: Mindset Sort

Have older students come up with examples of fixed-mindset and growth-mindset statements, actions, and behaviors they encounter in their daily lives. Each example will be written on a sticky note.

Create large charts with the following headings: School, Relationships, Extracurricular Activities/Hobbies, Work/Chores. Post charts around the room.

Students categorize the fixed- and growth-mindset sticky note examples they wrote into the four categories. A fixed-mindset example might be: "I'm not good enough to make the basketball team, so I won't try" (Extracurricular Activities); "I'm not really a math person" (School); "She lied to me, so I'll never trust her again" (Relationships); "If I don't know how to do something at work, I ask my boss to show me" (Work/Chores).

For younger students, create a chart with sample fixed- and growth-mindset statements and questions. Read the statements aloud to the class, and decide together if they're fixed- or growth-mindset statements or questions. Use this opportunity to explicitly teach about the fixed and growth mindsets. For example, for the first statement, "Smart people get things more easily than other people," talk to students about how we're all at different places in our learning, and everyone will eventually encounter struggle in the learning process. Students can also add their own statements to the visual.

SAMPLE DRAWING: Statement Chart

	Growth Mindset	Fixed Mindset
Smart people get things more easily than other people.		X
If you make a mistake, people will think you're not smart.		X
When my teacher comments on my work, it's so I can do better in the future.	X	
My brain can't change much.		X
If I work hard, I can make my brain grow stronger.	X	
Anyone can learn anything if they work hard.	X	
I can learn from my mistakes.	X	
Which mindset uses the word *yet*?	X	
Which mindset uses the word *can't*?		X
Getting better is more important than getting a good grade.	X	
ASK FOR STATEMENT/QUESTION IDEAS FROM STUDENTS.		

STEP 4: Optional Extension Activity

If you need to reinforce the difference between fixed and growth mindsets, consider creating a sorting activity like below.

For younger students:
Have small groups sort a set of fixed- and growth-mindset statement cards. Review each statement and discuss the mindset association.

For older students:
Have students sort cards in groups and then brainstorm growth-mindset statements to replace the fixed-mindset statements. For example, students might change "I'm not good at this" to "I need more practice at this."

Post a set of growth-mindset cards as a visual in the classroom. Discuss how you expect the community of learners to build their growth mindset through focused effort.

FIXED-MINDSET STATEMENT	GROWTH-MINDSET STATEMENT
Math is not my thing.	I can grow my brain.
I'm not good at this.	I need to change my strategy.
She's the smart kid in class.	My hard work and effort has paid off.
Scores mean more than growth.	I'm not there yet.
It's better to look smart than take risks.	People can change.
I will never be that smart.	A good attitude is important in learning.
I feel dumb if I'm corrected.	I'm a problem solver.

STEP 5: Action Journaling

Have students journal or draw a specific action they will take toward building their growth mindset. If students have a difficult time with this task, encourage them to think of a specific goal they would like to achieve, setbacks they may encounter, and ways they'll work to overcome failures.

Provide students an opportunity to share their action step and don't forget to include your own growth action!

STEP 6: Elaborate

Discuss the importance of creating a classroom environment in which everyone can learn. Explicitly share with students how each learner is on his or her own journey. Some are learning academic skills, some are working toward social goals, and still others are developing additional ways to challenge themselves.

STEP 7: Defining Classroom Culture

Brainstorm a list of growth-oriented classroom rules, expectations, and guidelines. Ask students for suggestions on guidelines that could help them develop their growth mindsets and encourage it in others. Examples may include: Don't laugh when someone makes a mistake. Remember, everyone can learn. Try a different strategy if you don't get something the first time. Don't be afraid to ask each other for help, and so forth.

STEP 8: Prepare to Launch Next Lesson, "Growing Your Brain"

Distribute a handout with sketches of two brains. Have students create a growth-mindset brain (decorated with statements and symbols characteristic of a growth mindset, as they understand it) and a fixed-mindset brain (decorated with statements and symbols characteristic of a fixed mindset, as they understand it).

SAMPLE DRAWING: Brain Sketch

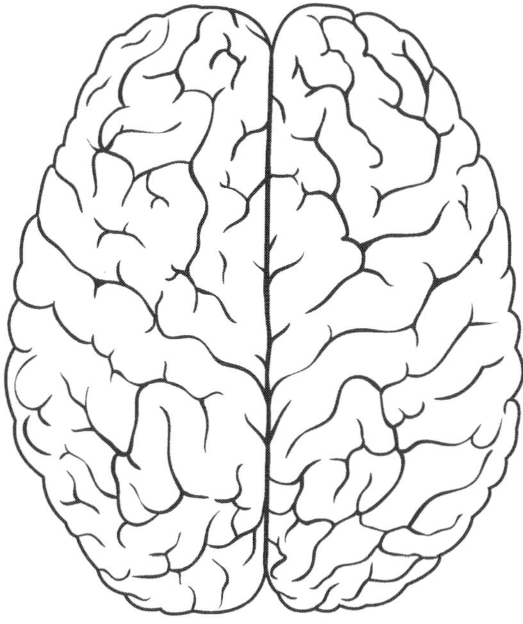

Make two copies of a blank brain sketch, like this one, and have students create a growth-mindset brain and a fixed-mindset brain by writing or drawing characteristics of each mindset, demonstrating their learning of the two types of mindsets.

STEP 9: Evaluate

- Students will collaborate to share and enhance their understanding of ideas and perspectives.
- Students will present information based on their drawings and discussions.
- Students will accurately describe information presented and connect to the classroom expectations and essential questions.

STEP 10: Feedback

Provide students with support and constructive feedback. Praise their effort in completing the tasks. Keep the praise on effort authentic and direct. For example, "I like how hard you worked on thinking of growth-mindset examples." Or, "You really stretched your brain adding creative details to your drawing."

Give yourself grace as you learn how to provide effective feedback to your students in your growth-mindset classroom. Remind your students that you too are learning and growing.

TEACHER JOURNAL: Reflection is a critical part of any lesson. Write a journal entry answering one or more of the following questions to determine what went well with your lesson and how it can improve next time.

- What went well with your lesson?
- How can you improve the lesson?
- What can you do as you prepare for the next month's lesson?
- What are your future goals with delivering growth-mindset lessons?

THE GROWTH-MINDSET ZONE

Establishing your classroom as a growth-mindset zone is an important part of making this your year of growth. Of course, when we say "growth-mindset zone," what we really mean is a judgment-free zone. As Dweck emphasizes in *Mindset*,[24] judging has little value, but engaging students in the learning process is key to growth. We recommend establishing guidelines that underpin the growth-mindset ethos of your class. Sharing those guidelines for growth with your students and making them part of the daily routine and classroom dialogue are essential to creating a growth-mindset zone.

Let's look at what establishing consistent classroom practices that convey the value of growth mindset to your students looks like. Mrs. H is a kindergarten teacher who has been teaching growth mindset in her classroom of five- and six-year-olds for the past several years. Read how she approaches teaching growth mindset to her students and then reinforces those skills in her classroom every day.

A PLACE OF GROWTH
MRS. H'S JOURNAL

In my class of kindergarteners, it is essential that I begin each school year establishing the expectation that we will resolve as individuals and as a community of learners to be the best problem solvers we can be. The most important rule in our classroom is to be prepared with a good learning attitude. The good learning attitude, of course, is the growth mindset. My students know a positive learning attitude will help them grow. We start our day by reciting a pledge establishing our classroom as a place of growth:

"Today I will:
Have a good learning attitude.
Be an active learner and grow my brain.
Be a mindful problem solver."

My students often remember things better when they are put with actions, so we have an action associated with each part of our pledge. "Have a good learning attitude!" is recited with an exaggerated wide smile and thumbs on cheeks as the students move their heads from side to side. "Be an active learner and grow my brain" is said as students place their hands over their heads and pantomime a growing brain. "Be a mindful problem solver" is said as students tap their heads with a pointer finger, the universal sign for thinking hard. Reciting these rules and doing their corresponding actions sets the tone for each day in class.

I spend a lot of time coaching students to understand that a good learning attitude includes embracing challenges, solving problems, and learning from mistakes. I model this attitude by sharing what it looks like to have a good learning attitude and what it looks like to not have a good learning attitude.

I do the same modeling with problem solving. It is important to explicitly teach this to students. They need to see examples of how to be a problem solver, learn problem-solving techniques, and celebrate their efforts in problem solving.

As part of this explicit instruction, I share what it looks like to NOT be a problem solver by treating the kids to a teacher tantrum at the beginning of each year. I stomp, cry, and pout when I can't figure something out. "This is too hard!" I'll say, as the students look at me in shock. "I can't do this!" Initially, the students are stunned by the fact their teacher is throwing herself on the floor and having a hissy fit. Once I have their attention, I ask them if there would have been a better way for me to handle the situation. (Some students beat me to the punch, coming to my aid to offer assistance before my tantrum demonstration is even over.) Of course, hands fly into the air, offering suggestions about how I can regain my positive learning attitude. I usually take this opportunity to brainstorm strategies for problem solving. Kids come up with ideas like:

- *Ask a peer or the teacher for assistance*
- *Look over the work from a previous lesson*
- *Try the problem again and again until you get it*
- *Think of another way to solve the problem*

I have found great value in building a classroom climate that teaches children to accept the learning place and pace of each learner. Students know that we are all working on growing our brains in different ways. Some students may be learning how to write the alphabet or recognize numbers, while others are working on what it means to be a good friend. Each of us has a job to be our best learner and to help those around us do the same. We do this by sharing our mistakes and strategies with each other, seeking help from peers, and using our growth mindsets.

FEATURES OF A GROWTH-ORIENTED CLASSROOM

Mrs. H doesn't just tell her students about growth mindset on day one and then leave it behind. She incorporates it into the daily routine of the classroom. And she'll tell you that over time, students start using that language in their interactions with each other. "Nothing is more satisfying," she says, "than hearing a student ask another student who is struggling, 'how can you be a mindful problem solver?'"

Like in Mrs. H's class, the culture of growth mindset should underlie your entire curriculum, but so too the physical space of your classroom. We're not suggesting that you hang signs demanding all who enter have a growth mindset or plaster the walls with posters of determined kittens. Rather, we're suggesting that you make some meaningful changes to your classroom environment that make it conducive to growth-oriented learning. It's entirely possible to convey growth-mindset messages through thoughtful choices in the display and arrangement of your classroom. Here are some ideas on how you can do it:

FEATURE	GROWTH-ORIENTED CLASSROOM	FIXED-ORIENTED CLASSROOM
STUDENT WORK DISPLAYS	Work displayed shows student effort—eraser marks, highlighted mistakes, and all.	Work displayed is flawless with no noticeable mistakes.
CLASS RULES	Positive classroom guidelines (like Mrs. H's) that reinforce the growth-mindset ethos are posted.	A long, comprehensive list of things students are not allowed to do is posted to outline the criteria of failure.
FURNITURE ARRANGEMENT	Students are situated collaboratively in groups or in arrangements from which groups can easily be assembled. Wheeled furniture can be a great classroom addition.	Desks face the front in rows and not easily grouped for collaborative work.

FEATURE	GROWTH-ORIENTED CLASSROOM	FIXED-ORIENTED CLASSROOM
WALL DISPLAYS/ DECOR	A favorite we've seen is "Change your words, change your mindset," featuring growth alternatives to fixed messages. For example, change "I'll never understand this" to "This challenging work is helping my brain grow." Another great sign: "Make mistakes."	Messages like "Practice makes perfect" and "You are great!" are problematic because practice doesn't always make perfect and not everyone is currently great at everything. Consider your messages through a growth-mindset lens; make sure they're purposeful.
TEACHER'S DESK	Teacher's desk is up front and easily accessible; better yet, there's no desk and the teacher moves throughout the classroom during the lesson to physically invite questions and demonstrate availability; teacher work is done in designated landing spaces.	Teacher's desk is in the back of the classroom, staring at the backs of student's heads, not inviting questions or interaction through eye contact and/or physical proximity.
ADDITIONAL SPACES	Includes seating like a couch or bean bags and other flexible spaces, as well as extra whiteboard space or lapboards so students can collaborate and work out ideas, or a "quiet area" where students can use noise-canceling headphones to focus on individual tasks. The growth-mindset classroom accounts for different learning styles and paces.	No thought put into additional spaces; everyone is given the same desk and expected to sit and work in the same manner. No extra consideration is given to different learning styles in the context of the classroom environment.
CLASSROOM MANAGEMENT	Discipline is private, personal, and done with dignity. Consider a coaching approach to discipline in favor of a punitive approach.	Names on the board with missing assignments published for the world to see. Behavior charts with big Xs for bad days or red cards.

The growth-mindset classroom environment should be space that communicates hard work is a value. It should place a premium on taking risks and tackling challenges, and communicate to students that this is a safe space in which to ask questions and make mistakes. It should value challenges—and the inevitable failure that comes with taking them on—and never emphasize perfection over effort.

INVOLVING PARENTS IN THE GROWTH-MINDSET GAME

While it's important the physical space of your classroom communicate those messages, it's also essential that you, as the classroom leader, support those messages in other ways. One of the most effective ways to reinforce the value of growth mindset in your classroom is by sending information home to parents. Sending a letter and literature on growth-mindset home at the beginning of the year will help parents understand that you're not a teacher who places a premium on test scores and grades; rather, the focus of your classroom is growth and improvement.

Here's a sample letter we've drafted to explain the growth mindset to parents and to give them some tools to extend it at home.

Dear Parent,

I am a firm believer in the power of the growth mindset, and approach each year with the belief that all my students are capable of learning and growth. What is growth mindset? Simply put, it is the belief that intelligence and ability are not fixed traits or that we are born with only so much of them. Rather, with effort and perseverance all students are capable of academic achievement.

Every day, your child will be immersed in the growth mindset in my classroom. My students will be asked to take educational risks. They will be praised not for their mental quickness or natural intelligence but for approaching the process of learning with grit and determination. And they will grow in ways they never thought possible.

But, here's the thing, these messages cannot only come from me, and so I am writing this letter to ask for your help. How can you help? You can value growth and improvement in your home. I am not a teacher who puts a high premium on scores and a number or letter at the top of a paper. Yes, grading is valuable as a data tool for tracking progress and helping me devise appropriate instruction, but the most important thing is that we see students grow. For example, if a student goes from scoring a 55 percent on an assessment to scoring a 68 percent, we have two choices. We can either look at the 68 percent as an unimpressive D+, or we can celebrate it as a big increase in comprehension of a skill or concept. I choose the latter. I'm not asking you to throw a party over a D+, but I am asking you to be mindful of where your students start and how they progress over time. In my estimation, continual progress, however incremental, is to be valued.

Here are some things you can do to extend and promote growth mindset in your home:

- *Encourage your child to take risks and tackle new challenges at school.*
- *Praise your child not for the ease with which he or she learns a concept but for the amount of effort put into learning it.*
- *Communicate with me if the material is too easy for your child, so we can offer him or her sufficiently difficult learning challenges.*
- *Emphasize perseverance and effort in extracurricular activities. For example, "I'm proud of how much effort you put into that basketball game" instead of "I'm proud of how many points you scored in that basketball game."*

I hope you'll commit to joining me on this growth-mindset journey. I cannot do it without your help. Please contact me if you have any questions or concerns.

Sincerely,

Your Child's Teacher

Including parents on your journey to instill growth-mindset beliefs in their children is absolutely crucial. After all, your growth-oriented work may easily come undone if a student goes home and hears only fixed-mindset messages. No, not every parent is going to jump on the bandwagon, but many will. You'd be surprised at the number of parents completely unaware of the fixed messages they've been sending their child.

In *Mindset,* Dweck writes, "No parent thinks, 'I wonder what I can do today to undermine my children, subvert their effort, turn them off to learning, and limit their achievement.' Of course not. They think, 'I would do anything, give anything, to make my children successful.'"[25] And, indeed, most parents we've encountered feel the same way, but they don't necessarily realize that some of the praise and feedback they're offering their children can be damaging and promote fixed mindsets. Quite the opposite: when parents say "Good job!" or "You're so smart!" they're trying to make their child feel good. In our experience, if you offer parents tools to praise and motivate their children in a healthier, more purposeful way, many of them are willing to take you up on it. One thing all parents have in common is that they want the best for their kids.

To keep up the growth-mindset dialogue with your parents, we recommend setting up some kind of system where you can offer them regular feedback on their student's growth. Survey parents at the beginning of the year and ask them in what areas they would like to see their child grow, or just update them on concepts or skills their student is working especially hard on, particularly if that hard work isn't necessarily reflected in high marks.

Here's an example of a take-home note for parents that reinforces growth as the primary goal of learning:

> A Growth Note About *Jack*
>
> *Jack has been working so hard on his math skills. He's gone from averaging a 65% to 76% on daily assignments and has a great learning attitude. I appreciate the effort that he is putting in, and I thought you should hear about it. Go Jack!*
>
> *-Ms. B*

EVEN MORE GROWTH MINDSET RESOURCES

As you seek to establish the growth-mindset ethos in your classroom and help parents implement it at home, you'll need an arsenal of resources. Here's a list of books, music, movies, and other resources that help teachers better understand growth mindset and offer students examples of what it looks like in practice.

BOOKS

Beautiful Oops, by Barney Saltzberg

The Dot, by Peter H. Reynolds

Everyone Can Learn to Ride a Bicycle, by Chris Raschka

If You Want to See a Whale, by Julie Fogliano

Ish, by Peter H. Reynolds

The Most Magnificent Thing, by Ashley Spires

Oh, the Places You'll Go, by Dr. Seuss

Rosie Revere, Engineer, by Andrea Beaty

Your Fantastic Elastic Brain: Stretch It, Shape It, by JoAnn Deak

MOVIES

Big Hero 6 (2014, Disney) [PG]

Cloudy with a Chance of Meatballs (2009, Sony Pictures Animation) [G]

Eddie the Eagle (2016, Marv Films) [PG-13]

Inside Out (2015, Disney Pixar) [PG]

Miracle (2004, Disney) [PG]

Rudy (1993, Tristar) [PG]

Spare Parts (2015, Pantelion Films) [PG-13]

Zootopia (2016, Disney) [PG]

VIDEO CLIPS/TV SHOWS

Austin's Butterfly: Building Excellence in Student Work (YouTube channel: Expeditionary Legendary)

Caine's Arcade (short film by Nirvan Mullick)

Growth Mindset for Students (video series by ClassDojo.com)

"The Power of Belief" (TED Talk by Eduardo Briceno)

"The Power of Believing that You Can Improve" (TED Talk by Carol Dweck)

"You Can Learn Anything" (Khan Academy)

SONGS

"The Climb," by Miley Cyrus

"Don't Give Up," performed by Bruno Mars on *Sesame Street*

"Fall Up," by Sus B

"Firework," by Katy Perry

"Power of Yet," performed by Janelle Monae on *Sesame Street*

"What I Am," performed by will.i.am on *Sesame Street*

If you continually model growth mindset, show authentic examples of it being used in the world, and value growth-mindset behavior in your classroom, you'll start to see it reflected in your students. If you claim to your students that you value growth mindset but continue to reward perfection over growth, the students will respond to the expectation of perfection. Remember, in the growth mindset, growth is the goal of learning, not getting it right the first time. Your students won't be perfect practitioners of growth mindset right away. Offer them your grace and kindness as they learn to use their growth mindsets, and don't forget to give yourself the same.

Now that you understand the difference between the mindsets, next month we'll delve into the science behind the mindsets. Scientists have a saying: "Neurons that fire together, wire together." Learning the ins and outs of the brain processes associated with learning is vital in establishing teaching practices that reinforce effort as a path to achievement.

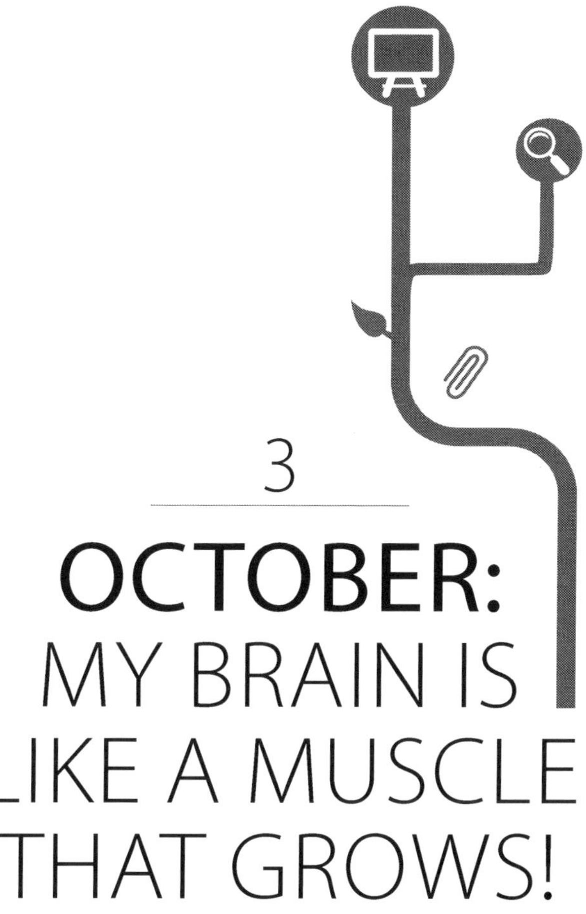

3

OCTOBER: MY BRAIN IS LIKE A MUSCLE THAT GROWS!

The measure of intelligence is the ability to change.

— Albert Einstein

OBJECTIVES

- ✓ Teach yourself and your students about neuroplasticity.
- ✓ Test and develop brain-based teaching strategies.

THE MATH BRAIN MYTH

A few weeks after taking the ACT—a college placement exam often administered in the Midwestern United States—Deb received her scores in the mail. On the math portion of the test, she got a nineteen out of thirty-six possible points, and on the reading portion she earned a thirty-two of thirty-six. What could possibly account for this disparity? How could Deb show such an aptitude in reading, earning a score in the ninetieth percentile among test-takers nationwide, and drop off so sharply in math? At first, Deb explained away the difference in her scores by saying that she simply wasn't a math person, but when she was pressed for her learning history in the two areas, a different picture emerged.

As a child, Deb was an unusually early reader. When she started school, she was rewarded for her talent by being complimented on her natural affinity for reading, called on to read aloud in class, asked to assist peers who were struggling in reading, and placed in high-ability reading groups. She spent her childhood weekends checking out books from the local library and devouring them by the dozen. When she got to middle and high school, she chose electives like drama, modern novel, journalism, and creative writing, where she could further her love of the written word. And when she got to college, what did she major in? You guessed it. English.

Her educational history in mathematics was an altogether different story. Deb remembers being a good math student early on, participating in, and even winning, extracurricular math competitions. In the fifth grade, she recalled her school assembling a math team to compete in a regional competition. She took the placement test, but didn't make the cut. After that, she goes a bit fuzzy. She remembers actively disliking math in middle school and taking only the required math courses in high school. After all, who would want to struggle through extra math classes like trigonometry and calculus, when they could shine in language-arts classes?

So, were Deb's ACT test scores an indication that she's not a "math person," as she initially said? Or were they a reflection of a learning history rich in language arts and deficient in mathematical instruction? Even though she believed that she was simply not a "math person," upon examining her history, she realized that it was the choices she made—and the challenges she avoided—that kept her from being a math person. She wasn't a math person because she never gave herself a chance to be one. She avoided the challenge of math because she was too busy cementing herself as a language superstar.

Deb isn't alone. Scores of people believe math aptitude is some sort of inborn genetic trait. "If you're not born a math person, you'll never be one." Don't believe us? Google the phrase "not a math person," and you'll net over seventy-thousand results!

OUR CHANGING BRAIN

The brain can grow and change in incredible ways when pushed. Like in Deb's case, the absence of practice and challenge in math stymied her brain's growth in that realm of study, while the constant practice and challenge in language arts helped her brain flourish. A wave of new research addressing the brain's plasticity — or its ability to change and grow and make new connections — has resulted in revelations that have upended long-held truths in the world of neuroscience.

New research reveals that humans, with dedicated effort and practice, are capable of making incredible, long-lasting changes to our brain throughout our lifetime. Here are a few examples:

- In a study published in the *Journal of Neuroscience*, it was found that brains of people who are born deaf essentially rewire so that the area of the brain typically reserved for processing sound instead assists with processing touch and vision.[26]
- The neuroscientist David Eagleman, author of *The Brain: The Story of You*, tells the story of Cameron Mott, who at four years of age had half her brain removed in an effort to counteract the effects of a rare disease. Cameron's brain "rewired" itself so that her half brain worked like a whole one, and today is "essentially indistinguishable" from her classmates.[27]
- The hippocampi (the part of the brain responsible for memory) of London cab drivers grew as they memorized over twenty-five thousand city streets in order to pass the city's cab licensing examination.[28]

Neuroplasticity, or brain plasticity, is the brain's ability to change itself throughout our lives. Like in the examples above, our brains even have the capability to rewire themselves to adapt to a situation.

Try to think about the brain like a muscle. Lifting weights and exercising muscles makes them stronger, right? In the same way, exercising our brain makes it stronger—when we learn new things, our brains actually become denser and heavier. Introduce your students to their brains with this mini-lesson.

MEET YOUR BRAIN

LESSON PLAN

OBJECTIVE

By the end of the lesson, students will be able to:

- explain the different parts of the brain.

RESOURCES AND MATERIALS

- Play-Doh (red, orange, purple, yellow, blue, green — or substitute other colors, as needed)
- White paper
- Writing utensils
- Example of a Play-Doh brain model. Make sure to have students build the brain on white copy paper or use sticky notes to label the various parts of the brain.

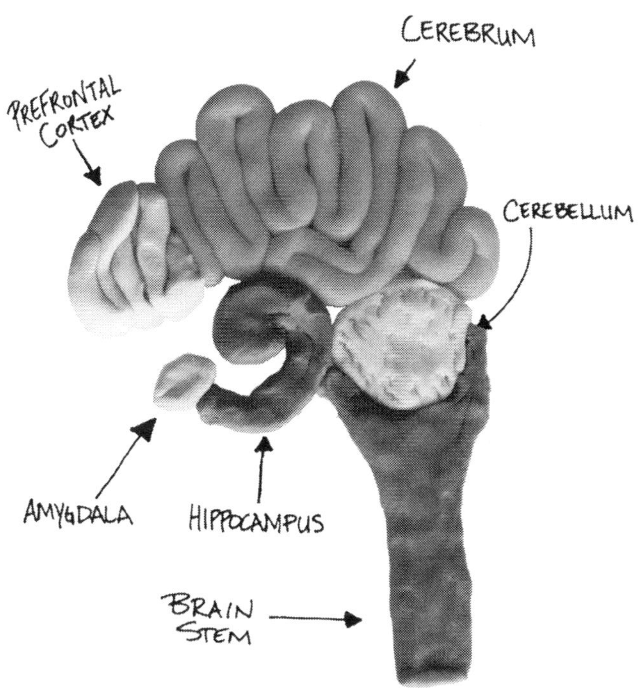

METHOD: MEET YOUR BRAIN

Divide students into small groups and redistribute the student sketches of the growth- and fixed-mindset brain sketches from the September lesson. Remind students that they decorated the brains with growth- and fixed-mindset statements and symbols as they understood it. Give students a few minutes to review and add any additional items to their brain sketches. Use the following questions to help generate group discussions.

- "Think of a time you learned something new. What steps did you take to learn it?"
- "Think of a time you failed at something. How did it make you feel? What happened after you failed?"

Share with students how the brain is an organ in our bodies that has an important job of helping us learn. Say, "Our brain has two hemispheres, the left and right. And each side is made up of different parts, including the cerebrum, prefrontal cortex, hippocampus, cerebellum, brain stem, and amygdala. All of these parts work together to help us learn and grow."

Next, pass out Play-Doh to each student (or group of students, depending on your supply of Play-Doh). Students will need a tub of blue, and smaller portions of orange, red, green, and yellow. Pass out a piece of white paper to each student, and have students build their brain models on the white paper.

Tell students that today they'll learn about the different parts of the brain and how those parts function. They'll be building a cross-section of the brain. In this activity, tell your students the name and function of various parts of the brain, as they mold each part out of Play-Doh or clay. By the end, they'll have created a cross-section model brain.

First, introduce the cerebrum.

CEREBRUM: Quick! What's 2 + 2? If you answered the question, you were using your cerebrum. You might recognize it as the wrinkly surface of the brain. The cerebrum is an important part of your brain, and also the biggest. It's the part you use for thinking! When you solve problems, draw pictures, or play games, you can bet your cerebrum is involved. Even your memories are stored here. (Expand as much or as little as is appropriate for your class on the functions of the cerebrum and the other parts of the brain. For younger students, keep it simple. For older students, give more detail about the functions of the various parts.)

Instruct the students to roll red Play-Doh into a long, snake-like shape as you're telling them about the cerebrum. Students will then swirl and twist the Play-Doh so it's good and wrinkly to create the cerebrum of their model. (See example on page 57.)

CEREBELLUM: Give your neighbor a high-five! Guess what? You couldn't give a high-five without help from a small part of the brain called the cerebellum. The cerebellum is located at the back of the brain. It has an important job in controlling our muscles. Our muscles help us run, jump, dance, and move in all sorts of ways, but they can't do it without a little help from the cerebellum. It's a little region that has a big job!

Have the students form their orange Play-Doh into a small mass with ridges and place it at the back of the brain model, similar to the example.

PREFRONTAL CORTEX: Give your forehead a little tap. (Model this.) Under the skin and bone on your forehead is the prefrontal cortex. This part of your brain is in charge of decisions. Bad or good, the choices you make come from your prefrontal cortex. When you think about pros and cons, compare and contrast choices, or consider different outcomes, you're using the prefrontal cortex.

Have the students roll the yellow Play-Doh in a snake-like piece, and then twist it and place it at the front of the brain. (See example.)

HIPPOCAMPUS: How do you know the way to the playground? (Allow for answers.) When we navigate to a certain place, like the playground, we are using our hippocampus. And it does more, like turning experiences into long-term memories.

Have students create a short, curved piece using purple Play-Doh. "Hippocampus" comes from Latin for "sea horse," so consider the curvy shape of a sea horse in making the hippocampus. Attach it under the cerebrum and to the left of the cerebellum. (See the sample Play-Doh brain on page 57.)

AMYGDALA: How are you feeling today? No matter how you feel, your emotions are all coming from the same place: the amygdala. The amygdala is a group of neurons deep inside your brain. The amygdala is like an emotional control center.

Have students use green Play-Doh to create an almond-shaped piece to attach to the base of the hippocampus. (See example on page 57.)

BRAIN STEM: Have you ever wondered how our bodies know to breathe while we're sleeping? You can thank the brain stem for that. In addition to helping send messages from the brain to other parts of the body, the brain stem is responsible for our involuntary functions (those are things the body does on its own without our help) like breathing, digesting food, or sneezing.

Have students use blue Play-Doh to create a trunk-like structure that extends from under the cerebellum downward to create a brain stem. (See example on page 57.)

Tell students that, using the piece of white copy paper on which they built their Play-Doh brain, they'll now label parts of their brain model and write examples of how they use the different parts of their brain.

Cerebrum: Label the red Play-Doh as the cerebrum, and write or draw an important thing they have learned in school.

Cerebellum: Label the orange Play-Doh as the cerebellum, and write or draw a sport or physical activities they enjoy doing.

Prefrontal cortex: Label the yellow Play-Doh as the prefrontal cortex, and write or draw a tough decision they have had to make.

Hippocampus: Label the purple Play-Doh as the hippocampus, and write or draw a picture of a special memory.

Amygdala: Label the green Play-Doh as the amygdala, and write or draw a picture of a time they felt very happy, scared, excited, frightened, and so forth.

Brain stem: Label the blue Play-Doh as the brain stem, and write or draw an involuntary reaction they have experienced (sneeze, cough, yawn, etc.).

CHECK FOR UNDERSTANDING

Check to make sure that students completed the models correctly. Have students photograph their creations to save and share.

BRAIN PLASTICITY

The brain's ability to change is called "plasticity." Inside our brains are billions of nerve cells called neurons. When you're using your brain, electrical signals are firing through a pathway called an axon. The signal is received by dendrites, little finger-like structures branching out from the neuron, and delivered to the cell body, where the signal can be sent out again to connect to another neuron. The more you learn, the more pathways between neurons you create. When a pathway is traveled often, it gets stronger. Lots of strong pathways in the brain mean neurons can send more and faster signals to one another—this means you're learning and remembering more and more things! You can remember this by teaching your students this rhyme: "Neurons that fire together, wire together." Everyone's brains have the capability to make connections and grow through practice and learning!

If students have trouble understanding this concept, offer them this metaphor. Pretend that you live in a wooded area, and each day you walk from your house down to a little stream. Over time, you have created a well-worn path through the woods from your house to the stream. Like this path, skills, knowledge, and habits that you often use are well-worn paths in your brain. You can easily do these things because the neuronal pathways are constantly used. But when you learn something new, you have to develop a new path.

Go back to the house in the woods for a moment. Let's say one day you spot a lovely meadow off the path. You decide that you'd like to get to it, but there's no clear way to get there. So you trudge through the brush, moving rocks, ducking limbs, and tripping on obstacles. You get there eventually, but it wasn't easy. It'll take time to wear a new path to the meadow as smooth as the path to the stream. When you learn something new, you're creating a new path in your brain; this is neuroplasticity. Anyone can make a new path, but it's hard work. And, just like a path in the woods, if you don't use the new paths in your brain often, they'll grow over and become difficult to navigate once again. That's why people sometimes say, "Use it or lose it!"

Learning about brain plasticity can help students put aside destructive ideas like people are born stupid, average, or smart, and embrace challenge as an integral and natural part of learning. It's taking on these new challenges outside our comfort zones where the biggest changes in the brain can be seen. To step outside one's comfort zone to start seeing these changes, one needs to first attack the new challenges, mistakes and all, with a growth mindset. When students understand how their brains learn, they can visualize the process happening in their heads as they take on new challenges.

Jo Boaler, a math education professor at Stanford University and author of *Mathematical Mindsets*, says that when students make a mistake in math, it triggers brain activity that isn't present when students get the right answer. "For people with a growth mindset, the act of making a mistake results in particularly significant brain growth," writes Boaler.[29]

So what does this mean for your students? First, subjects like math should be less about demonstrating mastery of concepts and more about learning. Boaler describes the distinction between math as a *performance subject*, in which students are given closed tasks and praised for coming up with right answers, and a *learning subject*, in which students are given open tasks and afforded the opportunity to work through the process of deeply learning without the constant need to answer questions correctly.[30]

WHY LEARNING BRAIN SCIENCE MATTERS

A critical, though often overlooked, aspect of teaching the growth mindset is teaching students just how their brains work. From the moment we're born we begin learning foundational skills in a variety of disciplines and areas—this learning forms the scaffold on which later skills and concepts will be constructed. After all, you wouldn't expect someone to read *The Scarlet Letter* who didn't know the alphabet, and you wouldn't ask someone to solve for X in a quadratic equation who wasn't familiar with the number system. But we routinely ask students to do the work of learning without ever teaching them how their brains will accomplish that work.

Dweck and her colleague Lisa Blackwell did a study with seventh graders who had been labeled "low achieving."[31] The whole group of seventh-grade students received instruction on study skills, and some of the students were also taught how the brain grows like a muscle. The students who received the extra information about how their brains can grow showed higher motivation in school and produced better math grades than their counterparts who didn't receive the training. Writing in *Principal Leadership*, Dweck shared a story of a young man who had made quite a show of clowning around with his friends, but after learning about how the brain can grow, he looked at the researchers and said, "You mean I don't have to be dumb?"[32] This story is an excellent example of how teaching growth mindset and brain science to students can help them see new possibilities for themselves.

If learning how the brain works made such an impact on these seventh graders, imagine the impact it could make in our teaching. Putting students aside for a moment, consider that many teachers are unfamiliar with the science behind how people learn, despite having dedicated their lives to the practice of it. In an informal poll of our colleagues, most teachers reported not having experienced any courses, or even units of study, on brain science during their undergraduate training. Most teachers who reported having studied how the brain learns as part of their teaching education did so in a master's-level program. As you work through the process of teaching students how their brains work, consider volunteering to present the topic at an in-service or otherwise sharing it with colleagues. This is invaluable information for teachers, too!

Teaching students about brain plasticity can make a huge difference in your year of growth mindset. It may be difficult to get students to buy into the somewhat abstract idea that belief in the potential of your skills, abilities, and intelligence to grow over time can increase achievement, but showing them the science behind how the brain works has the potential to turn doubters into believers. Teaching students about their cognitive processes has to be a nonnegotiable part of your mindset instruction. Luckily, neuroplasticity is a lesson that even our youngest students can learn. Remember Mrs. H's class? Her kindergarten students can tell you: the brain is like a muscle that grows! Let's take a look at a sample lesson on brain plasticity.

BRAIN PLASTICITY

LESSON PLAN

LEARNING OBJECTIVE

By the end of the lesson, students will be able to:

- explain the way we learn new things and grow our brains.

RESOURCES AND MATERIALS

- Twizzlers Pull 'n' Peel, Wikki Stix, or pipe cleaners
- Play-Doh
- Video projection equipment

METHOD

View a video, "How Neurons Communicate," describing how neurons make connections when we learn new things: https://youtu.be/hGDvvUNU-cw (video courtesy of BrainFacts.org on YouTube).

After the video, discuss with students how the brain learns new things and grows, and how challenging tasks and mistakes can help this process.

Tell students that today they'll be building a neuron. Explain to students that there are one billion neurons in their brain, and neurons are the building blocks of the brain. Neurons work together to help us do things. When we become very good at something, like solving a simple addition problem in math, for example, the neurons required for that process learn to quickly fire together. The more these neurons fire together, the more efficient the process becomes. That's why practicing makes things much easier. But when neurons have to do something out of the ordinary, like a long division problem, it takes longer for our brain to coordinate the process among our neurons. This is learning! With lots of practice our neurons can quickly make connections to do long division problems, and the process gets easier and easier. When we do challenging new work, we are making new connections in our brains between different neurons. Today, we're going to make a model of a neuron, so you can see the parts involved in making connections between neurons in your brains.

Students will create a model of a neuron by using Play-Doh and Twizzlers. Give each student two golf ball–sized mounds of Play-Doh and one rope of Pull 'n' Peel Twizzlers. Instruct students to create a cell body with one ball of dough and to make dendrites by rolling small amounts of the second ball of dough into long and short finger-like branches that extend from the cell body. Next, have students peel apart the Twizzlers. Tear one section into smaller pieces to arrange at the end of the axon to create the presynaptic terminals. The single, unbroken sections of Twizzler rope will act as the axon, the path the electrical currents travel. The more the path is traveled, the stronger it gets. Students will demonstrate this concept by adding a section of Twizzler rope for each of the following tasks:

- Instruct students to think of something new they've recently been introduced to and add one section of Twizzler extending from the cell body to represent the new learning.
- Students will add another Twizzler section to represent learning practice like completing homework on the skill.
- A third Twizzler section will be added to represent mistakes and challenges that are overcome in the learning process.
- The next section will be added to represent the demonstration of learning, like when students teach what they know, apply the skills correctly, or connect the skill to a new concept.
- Ask students to come up with examples of other ways they can strengthen their axon by adding sections of Twizzler.

Once the student has built a neuron model, they will use a dry erase marker or sticky notes to label the parts of the model. As the students label their models, describe how each part of the neuron works.

DENDRITES: These are the receivers. They receive incoming messages from other cells and send it into the cell body.

CELL BODY: The cell body generates an electrical signal to send the information to another cell.

AXON: Information travels down the axon away from the cell body toward the presynaptic terminal.

PRESYNAPTIC TERMINAL: Information moves between the presynaptic terminal and dendrites of another neuron through chemical signals.

Have students arrange models together to demonstrate how neurons connect to one another.

CHECK FOR UNDERSTANDING

Check to make sure students have a correct model of the neuron and encourage them to share their learning with a peer.

METHOD MIX-UP

Use these tools as a way to differentiate the product.

TOOLS	DESCRIPTION
AUGMENTED REALITY	Have students draw a neuron and record a video demonstrating their knowledge of how our brains grow. Use the Aurasma app (or other AR app) to scan the image and attach the augmented reality video to the drawing.
STOP-MOTION VIDEO	Have students use clay or Play-Doh to create a stop-motion video depicting the neuron connection process and add narration about how a neuron works. We recommend Stop Motion Studio from the App Store.
NARRATED VIDEO	Have students create a short video explaining how brain plasticity works. We recommend Adobe Voice. Students upload their own images or find pictures to illustrate the process.
BUILD A NEURON	Students can model their understanding of neuroplasticity by creating a neuron using Lego bricks or other building materials.
SKIT	Students write a skit to demonstrate how connections are made between neurons.
SONG OR POEM	Have students develop a song or poem to depict the neuron connections in the brain.
BLOG	Have students blog about their neuron connections. How are they growing their brain? What steps have they taken? Publishing student blogs is a great way to engage parents in the growth process happening in your classroom. Use the apps Kidblog or Seesaw for safe, secure student blogs.

BRAIN-CENTRIC TEACHING

Imagine how powerless students must feel at school if they've internalized the belief that there's nothing they can do to meaningfully change their intelligence. Once students understand that the brain is an ever-changing organ, they'll feel empowered to put in more effort and tackle new and difficult learning challenges because they'll finally understand it's hard work, not genetics, that dictate achievement. As we saw with Deb at the beginning of the chapter, the more students expose themselves to practice and challenging work, the more neural connections they'll make, and the stronger their cognition in that area of study.

We refer to "cognition" as the act of learning and "metacognition" as thinking about and monitoring that learning. Metacognition is, in essence, thinking about how we think. Metacognition, or "thinking awareness," is a cornerstone of a growth-oriented classroom and should be part of well-rounded instruction on how the brain learns. Thinking about our growth and fixed mindsets and how using different mindsets results in different outcomes falls under the umbrella of metacognition.

In fact, there's a wide range of metacognitive strategies teachers use to help students be the masters of their own brains. In many classrooms, students go through the motions of schoolwork. They read the study guide and pass the exam. They read the instructions and turn in a corresponding piece of work. But often, in these highly structured environments, students don't have the opportunity to plan their own approach to learning (it's already been done for them by the teacher), nor do they get time and space to reflect on the experience of learning (they've already moved on to the next topic). Metacognition is planning and reflecting about your own learning on a new plane of consciousness that many students aren't given the opportunity to access during the school day. Using metacognitive strategies of reflection and self-regulation requires students to step back and evaluate where they are and how they got there and where they need to be and how they can get there; it's also one of the most important life skills that our students are not being taught.

Just as we said that teaching students about growth and fixed mindsets is an intervention that has been proven to increase academic achievement, so too is teaching them about metacognition. Research has shown that students from preschool through college who have received explicit instruction in metacognition have been successful in using it, although the same research points out that metacognitive instruction is rarely used in the United States. Researchers also observed that students who learned that they had some agency over their brain using metacognitive strategies were more persistent and motivated as they tackled new learning challenges.[33]

As part of a growth-oriented classroom, teachers should encourage students to practice metacognition and become more strategic thinkers. Here are some strategies to guide students to deeper thinking:

Determine schema. Assess students' background knowledge using preassessments or self-assessments, or use strategies like K-W-L charts or anticipatory guides. Determine what students know and what connections they've made and still need to make. Prelearning activates thinking on prior knowledge and learning experiences related to the content.

Thinking stems. Post "thinking stems" students can use when talking through problems.

- I wonder . . .
- I'm learning . . .
- I'm thinking . . .
- I'm seeing . . .
- I'm feeling . . .
- I'm figuring out . . .
- This reminds of . . .
- I just learned . . .

Make sure that the thinking stems are easy to see, so students can access them from anywhere in the classroom.

Think sheets. Similar to thinking stems, but the sheets are printed on a worksheet for students to fill out instead of posted for students to think about. When students fill out a think sheet, they get a valuable opportunity to think about their thinking.

Journaling. Students journal reflections on units of study or projects; journaling gives students time to think about the thinking they did while completing a task. Having students free-write on their thinking processes may help them uncover information on their approach to learning they hadn't considered before.

Model metacognition. The teacher verbally talks through the metacognitive process to model it. Constantly referencing your own thinking processes helps students see the value of metacognition. You might say something like, "I'm thinking there is an error in this sentence, because I know that every sentence needs a subject and a predicate. I wonder if I can add a predicate to make this a complete sentence."

Risk-free environment. Create a classroom environment in which metacognition is valued as a learning tool. The expectation that students must talk through their learning process removes the vulnerability associated with it.

Encourage notations. Encourage students to write annotations and marginalia whenever possible. This can be done with paper and pencil or using digital annotation tools. By jotting down notes as they read, from questions on vocabulary to thoughts on character development, students will engage with the text (and their thoughts regarding it) more deeply.

BRAIN-BOOSTING ACTIVITIES

It turns out the human brain really likes an unexpected stimulus.[34] Our brains are wired to respond to stimuli in our environment that are out of the ordinary, which is why lectures and monotonous classwork can be ineffectual in engaging students' brains in learning. One way teachers are creating these elements of surprise and invigoration in the classroom is through brain boosts. A brain boost is an opportunity to step away from the task you're working on to engage in a whole body, kinesthetic activity that gets students reinvigorated and reenergized. Exercise results in more oxygen in the brain, and neurons fire more rapidly in an oxygen-rich environment. We like to tell our students, "Whew! Our neurons have been working so hard making new connections, they need to energize. Time for a brain boost!"

Here are some ideas for short brain boosts in class. Make sure to use your brain language as you engage students in brain boosts to reinforce the importance of exercising the brain.

Human knot. Give your students a break by using this fun, team-building activity. The students stand in a circle and grasp right hands with a person not standing next to them, and then do the same with the left hands. This creates the "human knot." Now the students have to untangle themselves without letting go. This fun and challenging problem-solving activity is great when your class needs a brain break and a boost in team spirit.

Air writing. Have the students stand up. Ask them a series of questions — content relevant or just for fun — which they'll answer by "writing" in the air with their pointer finger.

Junk drawer. This improvisational game was featured on *Whose Line Is It Anyway?* Keep a bag full of odds and ends: a pool noodle, spatula, foam finger, pipe cleaner, etc. Ask students to reach into the bag, pull out an item, and then come up with an inventive way to use the item that was not intended by its maker. For example, the pool noodle becomes a prosthetic elephant trunk.

Yoga break. Learn some simple yoga poses to share with your classes during a brain boost. A simple restorative pose with focused breathing is a great way to reenergize students. Try Upward Facing Dog, Warrior Pose, and Tree Pose to get started!

YouTube brain breaks. YouTube has a ton of videos for guided brain boosts. Keep a video playlist handy for those moments when you need to fight the fidget, but you have nothing planned. Just search "brain breaks" and you'll find thousands of videos. A word of caution, preview the videos first to make sure that they're appropriate for your class.

4

NOVEMBER: I AM A VALUED MEMBER OF THIS LEARNING COMMUNITY

We rise by lifting others.

— Robert Ingersoll

OBJECTIVES

- ✓ Develop strategies to build relationships with students.
- ✓ Develop strategies to build relationships with parents.
- ✓ Develop strategies to build relationships with colleagues.

WHY RELATIONSHIPS MATTER

In the popular 2013 TED Talk "Every Kid Needs a Champion," the veteran educator Rita Pierson told this story of an exchange with another teacher:

"A colleague said to me one time, 'They don't pay me to like the kids. They pay me to teach a lesson. The kids should learn it. I should teach it, they should learn it. Case closed.' Well, I said to her, 'You know, kids don't learn from people they don't like.'"[35]

Pierson's assertion that kids do not learn from unlikable teachers is not just the commonsense observation of an experienced educator; it's backed up by research. One study suggested positive teacher-student relationships, particularly for students labeled academically at risk, have a beneficial impact on students' academic efforts and are associated with higher confidence in academic ability, both of which contribute to higher overall achievement.[36] Another study indicated positive student-teacher relationships can improve students' relationships with one another, as well as increase engagement in their schoolwork.[37]

We have said that growth mindset is simply the belief that things like intelligence and ability can be changed. Full stop. So, you may find yourself asking, what do relationships have to do with it? After all, only *you* can control *your* mindset, right?

Well, yes and no. While it's true only an individual can change his or her own mindset, we believe that through developing strong relationships it's possible to foster a classroom environment in which conditions are ripe for students to embrace a growth mindset. In *Mindset,* Carol Dweck discusses how teachers who offer appropriate, targeted praise can foster a growth mindset in students. We believe that this is just one way teachers can foster a growth mindset. In fact, there are many ways teachers can affect the mindsets of the students, colleagues, and parents with whom they work, and the best place to start is in laying a foundation on which strong relationships can be built.

RELATIONSHIP SELF-ASSESSMENT

Take this relationship self-assessment by indicating a yes or no reaction to each statement. This will help you determine if you tend toward a growth or fixed mindset in regard to school relationships.

I usually give students tasks in which I know they can succeed. YES or NO

I prefer not to share personal details about my life with my students. YES or NO

My main job is to lead instruction. YES or NO

Students' personal lives are none of my business. YES or NO

Unless there's a problem, I don't need to communicate with parents. YES or NO

I have little patience for helicopter parents. YES or NO

I don't go to work to make friends; I go to work to do my job. YES or NO

What other teachers are doing in their classrooms doesn't affect me. YES or NO

If parents don't show up to conferences, they probably don't care about their student's education. YES or NO

My administrator only observes me a few times a year, so I don't pay much attention to the feedback. YES or NO

SELF-ASSESSMENT RESULTS

If you said no to most of the statements, it's likely that you have a growth-mindset approach to networking and making connections with students, parents, and colleagues. If you said yes to three or more of the questions, you'll need to be extra intentional about developing meaningful relationships with students and other school stakeholders.

In this chapter, we discuss strategies for formulating meaningful, mutually beneficial relationships with students, parents, and colleagues.

THE VALUE OF STUDENT-TEACHER RELATIONSHIPS

So why is a growth-mindset attitude toward relationship building critical to the achievement of your students? Because any teacher who's been in the business long will tell you Pierson *is* right, students simply don't learn as much from teachers they don't like. If you want students to develop a growth mindset and believe in their ability to achieve at high levels with hard work and perseverance, they have to know that you believe they can make it happen.

In her TED Talk, Pierson relates another tactic she uses to champion her students, in which she and her students say this mantra together: "I am somebody. I was somebody when I came. I'll be a better somebody when I leave. I am powerful, and I am strong. I deserve the education that I get here. I have things to do, people to impress, and places to go."[38] Implicit in this mantra is the ethos of the growth mindset. Pierson reminds her students not only is it a possibility they'll improve but, to her, it's a given. She believes that if this type of mantra is repeated enough, it becomes a part of the student's life.

Students in the fixed mindset are fearful of and anxious about appearing stupid in front of teachers and classmates. They want everyone to know how smart they are at all times, which is why they tend to avoid challenges at which they may fail. Stepping out of the fixed mindset and into the growth mindset takes vulnerability on the part of students, and it's likely they won't be willing to show that kind of vulnerability to just anyone. But for a teacher who trusts and respects them, wants the best for them, and won't judge them when they make a mistake, they just may be willing to take the leap.

GROWTH-ORIENTED STUDENT-TEACHER RELATIONSHIPS

Building strong relationships with your students is key to letting them know that they're valued members of the learning community in the classroom and school. Here are the five cornerstones of our approach to effective relationship building with students.

- Students know that the teacher has faith in their ability to achieve.
- Students respect and like their teacher as a person.
- Students seek and embrace the teacher's feedback.
- Students know that grades are less important than growth.
- Students feel safe with their teacher.

Students know that the teacher has faith in their ability to achieve. The crux of the growth mindset is that students must believe in their own ability to achieve at high levels with grit and determination. But imagine how difficult it would be to believe that of yourself if you thought that your teacher didn't feel the same way. If you expect your students to have faith in themselves to grow, they must sense that you genuinely, enthusiastically believe in them, too. Remind students daily that you believe in their ability to achieve, and whether it's through process praise on a task well done or detailed improvement feedback, there are chances to practice this each day.

Students respect and like their teacher as a person. The best way to forge deeper relationships with your students is to take a personal interest in their lives and well-being. Take time to get to know your students' out-of-school interests. These private, non-school-related chats can also give you insights into other things going on in a student's life: parents are getting divorced; the student is dealing with an illness or diagnosis; the student has a parent absent or in prison. Students come from all kinds of circumstances and backgrounds; the more information you have about each of your students, the deeper you can build your relationships and better tailor a learning experience most beneficial to them. Likewise, sharing appropriate, personal information with your students—like how you struggled with Algebra II or what you plan to do over the weekend—will forge deeper mutual relationships.

Students seek and embrace the teacher's feedback. In strong student-teacher relationships, students do not get defensive in the face of critical feedback but recognize it as part of the process of improvement and growth. When students believe that you have their best interest at heart, they'll respond to feedback in more productive ways. Make it clear to students that their growth is your main priority, and let them know that the purpose of constructive feedback is to help them improve. If students have difficulty accepting feedback in positive ways, it may be a signal that you need to work on relationship building so students know that your feedback comes from a place of caring and support, not judgment. In that case, pulling them aside for a one-on-one chat to explain the feedback in more detail or scheduling a conference to work through the changes together can show the student that you're a source of support. You'll know that you've hit your stride when students (even ones who aren't in your class anymore) approach you asking for honest feedback on their work.

Students know that grades are less important than growth. In strong student-teacher relationships, you've set goals for your students and helped them set goals for themselves. Students know grading is part of the process and a source of data you use to track their overall performance, but they also recognize the most important thing to you is their progression toward the goals you've set together. You should keep an open dialogue about overcoming challenges and obstacles, and while grades should matter to you, the letter grade, in itself, should never hold more value than the progress it indicates. Allowing students multiple opportunities to learn material and achieve a better grade is an excellent way to demonstrate this belief to students.

Students feel safe with their teacher. Jacqueline Zeller, a former teacher and Harvard Graduate School of Education researcher, says that the social-emotional aspects of school, like relationships with teachers, are not unrelated to academic achievement; rather, the two are deeply connected. "When children feel more secure at school," says Zeller, "they are more prepared to learn."[39]

Students should feel completely safe in your classroom and in your presence. You should strive to be a source of support, not a source of anguish. Students should know, unequivocally, that you want what's best for them, you'll protect them, and you'll unconditionally care for them no matter what mistakes they make. We know in a growth mindset, mistakes are valued as learning opportunities. This goes for social-emotional mistakes, as well. If a student makes a poor choice, acknowledge the choice and deal with it privately and professionally, but continue offering support, encouragement, and kindness. Never hold a grudge against a student.

SMART goals. Write two goals that are Specific, Measurable, Attainable, Realistic, and Timely, and focus on improving your student-teacher relationships. For example, every day this week, I'll spend two minutes talking with a student on a non-school-related topic.

Relationship SMART Goal 1: ____

____

____

Relationship SMART Goal 2: ____

____

____

RELATIONSHIP-BUILDING STRATEGIES

Nina May's kindergarten teacher had a large circular rug with the letters of the alphabet printed on it. On the first day of school her teacher asked the students to each sit on the letter that started their last name. Nina beelined to the letter M, where she saw her classmate Katie already hunkered down. Surely, Katie must have made a mistake, Nina thought. But no, Katie was a letter M, too! When the girls realized that their last names started with the same letter, it was as if a most unusual coincidence had occurred. They were thrilled to have this special detail in common. Later Nina would be relocated to letter X (for organizational purposes), but her and Katie's friendship was cemented.

You've probably witnessed a similar scenario, something like: "I like Barbies!" "I like Barbies, too!" "Let's be best friends!" Sound familiar? Hunter Gehlbach, along with a team of researchers from Harvard's Graduate School of Education, wanted to explore the idea that people often associate positive feelings with those with whom they have things in common.[40] Gehlbach and his team wanted to know, specifically, whether student-teacher relationships could be enhanced by what they called "social perspective taking," through identifying commonalities in interests or values. In other words, if a student and teacher were to discover a mutual obsession with the *Star Wars* franchise, could the commonality positively affect their relationship?

Gehlbach and his team gave freshman students and their teachers a survey asking them to identify their interests, values, and learning preferences. Then they selectively shared the results with the students and teachers in a way that highlighted similar interests and values between the teachers and individual students.

"Our findings suggested the intervention was most effective in improving teachers' relationships with these [primarily black and Latino] historically underserved students,"[41] says Gehlbach, who goes on to explain that the intervention helped close an achievement gap of the underserved students as their grades went up. Gehlbach's findings indicated that the intervention was successful particularly in improving teachers' relationships with students, and that grades of black and Latino students, in particular, experienced a noted increase after the intervention.

How could such a simple intervention like revealing commonalities between teachers and students result in increased academic achievement? Well, for one, it gives the teacher opportunities to talk about non-school-related topics with students as a relationship-building strategy. This information could also help teachers tailor learning activities to incorporate some of the student's personal interests, resulting in increased engagement on the student's part. Gehlbach also theorizes it helps teachers see students as individuals with different needs and interests, which could affect teacher attitudes toward students.

One way to attempt to achieve Gehlbach's results is by giving your students getting-to-know-you activities and inventories at the beginning of the year. Making efforts to get to know your students demonstrates that you're interested in who the students are as individuals and is much more engaging than the long list of don'ts, can'ts, shouldn'ts, and won'ts that students are often subjected to during first-day proceedings. But efforts to get to know your students shouldn't end on the first day.

Here are some additional activities and strategies teachers can use to build stronger connections with students.

Finding common ground. Take time at the beginning of the year to find things you have in common with your students on a personal level. Use those commonalities to strengthen your relationship.

Lunch buddies. Schedule individual lunch dates with your students. It's a great way to get one-on-one time with them to work on building your relationship.

Two-minute check-ins. Before school, after school, and during breaks, make it your goal to approach a student (particularly one who is struggling) and talk for two minutes about non-school-related topics. These short conversations can give you invaluable insight into your students' lives.

Just say yes. Make it a point to say "yes" to students requests as often as you can. Giving students some ownership over their work can help invest them in it. Even saying yes to small requests like "Can I use a green pen on this assignment?" can go a long way. Voice and choice is an excellent motivator.

Meet them at the door. An oldie, but a goodie! Try to personally greet each of your students as they come through your classroom door. Your smile and friendly greeting will help set the tone for a productive class.

Get-to-know-you activities. Take time out, especially at the beginning of the year, to engage students in activities focused on helping everyone get to know each other better. These activities help build up a strong class bond, which will benefit you and the class as you grow together.

Hand signals and code words. Instead of yelling at students to "sit down" or "be quiet," establish hand signals or code words at the beginning of the year that communicate these and other common instructions. This is a far more positive way to interact with students than trying to yell above the noise of learning.

Golden rule teaching. Treat students the way you want to be treated. Sounds pretty simple, right? But many teachers take their authority over students too far. Ensure that you're not being mean, overly disciplinary, or dictatorial by establishing yourself as a golden rule teacher. Go ahead and set rules for the kids, but hold yourself to the same standards—and be okay when students call you out on breaking them.

Forget the shop talk. Make an effort to talk to students about non-school-related subjects. Find out what extracurricular activities they're participating in, and use this knowledge to your advantage. "How was the art show this weekend?" "Three touchdowns? You were working hard in the football game on Friday!" These little asides let students know that you know they have things going on outside your classroom, and you care about those things, too.

Let's take a look at a few of these strategies in practice.

THE TWO-MINUTE CHECK-IN
MRS. H'S JOURNAL

Spending two minutes each day engaging students in conversation can have a powerful impact on building better student relationships. This strategy has served to help me learn more about my students' interests, build trusting relationships, improve classroom management, and curb attention-seeking behaviors.

I try to incorporate these check-ins throughout my day. Every morning before school I spend about fifteen minutes checking in with students while they eat breakfast, read a book, or walk to the classroom. I seek out conversations with students on the playground during recess, in line for the bus, or at lunch. I reserve the first ten minutes of our class time each day to connect with students as they check in and complete our morning routine.

These regular check-in times give me an opportunity to learn more about my students. I can easily get a feel as to whether they're having a great start to their day or if something is bothering them. I can use this information for continued relationship building in our classroom. I ask simple questions to get conversations started. What is your favorite food? What is your favorite color? What did you do last night? Do you like sunny weather or rainy weather? If you could be any animal, what would you be and why? These may seem like superficial topics, but often they serve as a gateway for meaningful conversation. I intentionally make eye contact and actively and authentically engage with the student to whom I'm speaking. If the student doesn't want to talk, then I check in at a later time.

This two-minute check-in period has created many opportunities for me to learn more about the students in our school. Building a trusting rapport with students allows me to coach them to make safe, respectful, and responsible choices. I demonstrate that I care about them and their role as a learner in our school community.

I have found that it's especially helpful to connect with those students who may act out with negative behaviors. My goal is to provide support, offer words of encouragement, foster growth mindsets, and interact with students in a manner that lets them know that I genuinely care about them. This allows me to connect with students, effectively address any concerns, or help alter behaviors that interfere with learning.

Meaningful relationships are at the core of building a positive school culture and a nurturing learning environment in which students can be empowered to achieve. The two-minute check-in is a great way to start building and establishing growth-oriented relationships with students.

THE VALUE OF GOLDEN RULE TEACHING
MS. B'S JOURNAL

As a brand-new teacher, I often found myself scrambling to get ready for my first class of the day. My homeroom students would see me streaking in just as the bell rang (and sometimes after), clutching hot-off-the-press copies and out of breath from my mad dash down the hall. A few months into the school year, a student walked in late to first hour, and I issued a tardy slip.

"That's not fair," the student said.

"Sorry you feel that way," I said, "but a rule is a rule."

"Then why do you always break it?" he asked.

He had me there.

As I stood in front of the class munching on the piece of humble pie my student had just served up, I understood that a strong teacher-student relationship, one in which I was the role model and earned the trust and respect of my students, could never be achieved with a "do as I say and not as I do" approach. This student likely didn't know it was my first year teaching. He didn't know that I had probably stayed up until midnight working on this lesson plan. He didn't know that I had small children at home, and often felt in that first year I was hanging on by a thread. All he saw was that I had set one standard for myself, and another for him. And he was right; it wasn't fair.

"You're right," I told him. "I'll let you off the hook, if you let me off the hook. And from now on we'll all do better being on time and ready to learn."

Later, as I reflected on this exchange, I saw how it could have gone a completely different direction. If I had stood my ground that the tardy rule applied to the student but not to me, I would have exercised my authority and won the argument, but sacrificed any respect I had managed to earn from my students in the process. Instead, I looked on the experience as an opportunity for growth. I asked myself:

- *How can I be better prepared for school each morning?*
- *What are ways I can better show my students I respect and care for them?*
- *How can I better model my expectations to my students?*
- *How can I set classroom rules and limits while still valuing my students as autonomous people with different individual needs?*

Asking these "how" questions was a great way to begin turning my values into concrete, achievable outcomes. These questions were my growth mindset talking. "Can" questions tend to invoke the fixed mindset, but "how" questions force me to come up with solutions to my problems instead of excuses for them. I realized that even though my students and I had different roles in the classroom, we all had a certain standard of behavior to live up to, me included.

THE NURTURED CLASSROOM

In this chapter, we've focused on strategies you can use to improve relationships with your students. Students' belief in your care and respect for them is a critical ingredient in the recipe for a growth-oriented classroom. If students don't like you, as Pierson tells us, they aren't going to learn from you. If you want students to internalize your growth-mindset messages, it's important that they trust the source.

Students also learn better when they're in a safe and nurturing environment. Does this mean that you need to throw all the rules out the window? Or coddle the students and handle their self-esteem with kid gloves? Not at all. It means that in order for students to get down to the real business of learning, with all its mistakes and failures and pitfalls and humbling setbacks, it must be done in a nurturing environment. Let's see what a nurturing environment looks like.

THE CODDLED CLASSROOM	THE NURTURED CLASSROOM	THE DISCONNECTED CLASSROOM
Mistakes are overlooked and have no real consequences.	Mistakes are learning opportunities followed by second (or third) chances.	Mistakes result in disciplinary action and/or loss of arbitrary points.
The students love the teacher because he or she lets them do what they want.	The students love the teacher because he or she encourages them to challenge themselves and is responsive to student needs.	Students view the teacher as an authoritarian figure/gatekeeper.
Teacher believes some students just aren't cut out for some subjects, and that's okay!	Teacher believes with effort and practice, every student can make achievement gains in any discipline.	Teacher believes as long as they pass the test, who cares?
Students are helpless and need to be closely managed through the learning process.	Students manage their own learning and are encouraged to take risks. Teacher serves as a facilitator and guide.	Students do what the teacher says; if they don't, they're noncompliant. If they do, they're "good students."

Are you creating the conditions for a nurturing classroom? If students feel that their teacher is too cavalier about their achievement or doesn't think that they can handle a challenge or, conversely, that their teacher is too focused on compliance and test scores, students may not feel that conditions are right to engage in real learning, mistakes and all. The sweet spot is the responsive teacher—one who provides appropriate challenges and responds to student needs. Your students' growth mindsets will have the most room to flourish in the nurtured classroom, where they're given big challenges and room to make mistakes as they conquer them.

Write three adjustments you could make to your classroom to build a more nurturing environment. For example: I could replace some chairs with yoga balls to help students who fidget release energy while working.

1. ______________________________

____

____

2. ______________________________

____

____

3. ______________________________

____

____

BUILDING POSITIVE RELATIONSHIPS WITH PARENTS

Relationship-building efforts should extend beyond your students. There's no question parental involvement in a student's education has positive effects. As teachers, we know parents matter. Many teachers, especially those with a fixed mindset, might write off some parents as disinterested or placing a low value on education simply because they missed a parent-teacher conference or forgot to sign the reading log (again). At the same time teachers are reporting an increase in unsupportive and disinterested parents, a recent National School Public Relations Poll said 66 percent of parents complained that teachers are not keeping them informed about what's happening in the classroom.[42] In other words, teachers are saying parents don't want information, and parents are saying teachers won't give it to them.

So, how can we rectify this obvious disconnect?

A teacher with a growth mindset makes efforts to get parents interested in their student's educational journey. He or she knows that all parents, guardians, and caretakers have the potential and capacity to positively affect a student's educational outcomes, and seeks to find ways to make it happen, no matter how limited the circumstances may seem. And studies suggest it's easier than you'd imagine.

In 2014, Harvard researchers conducted a field experiment in which teachers of students in a credit recovery program—students who have failed to earn the requisite credits for graduation—sent a brief message to parents each week about their student's performance at school.[43] Some parents received positive messages focused on what the student was doing well, while others received growth-oriented messages telling parents the areas in which their student could use improvement.

The likelihood a student would earn the credit they were attempting to recover increased by 6.5 percent when the parent received a weekly message, which decreased the overall failure rate by 41 percent. The students whose parents received the improvement messages—those focused on what the student could do better—had the most gains, as the students were 9 percent more likely to earn the credit they were seeking.[44]

So what does this research tell us? First, effective communication with parents doesn't have to be a protracted, face-to-face conference in order to make a difference. In the study, teachers sent short text messages to parents just once per week, and it had a significant effect on the achievement of the at-risk students. What's more, it's not necessary to shower the parents with praise of their child, just letting them know where their student can improve actually garnered better results. We've met teachers whose strategy is to "sandwich" growth messages in between compliments.

"Derrick is a great friend to his peers and goes out of his way to be kind to them. He currently has a failing grade in math because he routinely does not turn in his assignments. But he is a joy to have in class, and I love his fun personality!"

It's commendable to want to offer parents their dose of bad news wrapped in a larger helping of good news. It's kind of like hiding a dog's medication in the middle of a steak. The dog gets the medicine, but is none the wiser. Likewise, the parents get the improvement message, but it's so watered down they may not realize that you've given it to them.

Can you see the mixed signals Derrick's parents are getting with this style of feedback? The information about Derrick's lack of accountability when it comes to his math assignments gets lost in the middle of the noisy praise. Does this mean that you shouldn't praise children to their parents? No, it's important that parents know what their children do well, but, as research shows us, it's more beneficial to student achievement that they know where their children need to improve. It's important that you're clear and explicit when conveying messages of improvement.

Consider setting up a growth-oriented communication system at the beginning of the school year, like the one in the Harvard study. Here's an example of how you could start a similar communication system:

First, let the parents in on your plan, communicating to them the value of growth-oriented messaging.

Dear Parents,

It's very important to me that we are partners in your child's educational journey. I believe that the best thing I can do to assist you in your role on this journey is to let you know when your student needs encouragement in focusing on an area of his or her schoolwork in which he or she may be struggling. That's why you'll be receiving a weekly Growth Message from me.

Each week you'll receive a message highlighting an area in which your student could use improvement. Use the information to encourage your student to work harder and learn from his or her mistakes in that area. I'll have plenty of feedback on all the great things your student is doing in class, as well! But the Growth Messages will center on areas in which they need extra encouragement to tackle challenges.

HERE'S A SAMPLE GROWTH MESSAGE:

Erica has found our new unit on fractions quite challenging. She would benefit from regular practice and extra instruction in the area of fractions at home.

And here are some ways you might respond:

Offer Erica help on her math homework (or find a friend or relative who can).

Encourage Erica to approach me for extra help before or after school.

Provide words of encouragement to Erica as she tackles this new learning challenge. For example, "I appreciate how much effort you are putting into learning fractions." Or "I had trouble with fractions too, but if you keep working hard you'll get it, just like I did."

Provide Erica with some extra resources to reinforce fractions instruction at home. For example, download an app to her tablet that helps her practice fractions.

The goal of the Growth Messages is not to punish students for not doing well in a certain area; rather, it is to partner together to offer messages of encouragement and reinforce hard work and dedication as your student strives to learn a challenging concept. Remember, if students aren't being challenged, they aren't learning up to their potential! I strongly believe parents play a key role in their child's education, and Growth Messages are my way of strengthening our partnership in ensuring that your child has the best learning experience possible.

Sincerely,
Your Child's Teacher

As a teacher, part of your job is to coach parents. Most parents don't have an education degree; they need guidance on how to help their children. This doesn't mean that you have to spend exhaustive hours e-mailing, meeting with, and talking to parents. Rather, let your expectations for parent involvement be known at the beginning of the year. Let them know how you plan to involve them in their child's education, and give them explicit instruction on ways they can be a positive part of the process.

It's important to instill self-efficacy in children early on. They should understand the perils associated with an over-reliance on praise and perfection. As Dweck writes in *Mindset*, "If parents want to give their children a gift, the best thing they can do is to teach their children to love challenges, be intrigued by mistakes, enjoy effort, and keep on learning."

Using some simple strategies, teachers can facilitate the kind of growth-oriented relationship between parent and child Dweck describes. Here are some more ideas for establishing open lines of communication with parents. Use these tools to let parents know what's happening in the classroom so those values and concepts can be reinforced in the home.

STRATEGIES FOR COMMUNICATING WITH PARENTS

In terms of cultivating growth mindsets in your classroom, connecting and building relationships with parents can make all the difference for some students. Try some of these strategies:

Remind. Use this texting app to safely communicate messages to parents from your mobile device.

Newsletter. Use digital or paper newsletters to highlight ongoing learning. Use this opportunity for in-depth coaching to help parents try new strategies at home.

Social media. Set up a hashtag for your students (e.g., #Fabulous4thGrade or #SmithGrade6), as a way for parents to see what your class is doing via social media platforms like Twitter, Instagram, and Facebook.

E-Conferences. Having a hard time scheduling a face-to-face with a parent? Use Google Hangouts, Skype, or FaceTime to connect online.

Class channel. Give parents the opportunity to peek into what's happening in the classroom by setting up a video channel via YouTube or other video platform.

Polls and surveys. Constantly check for cooperation and understanding of your methods via polls and surveys. There are many free options, like Google Forms, for sending out polls and surveys and quickly aggregating results.

Kidblog or Seesaw. Allow your students an opportunity to share their learning by blogging about activities, challenges, mistakes, and successes they experience in the classroom.

Adobe Voice. Encourage students to create simple presentations to share their learning. Students can upload photos, text, and audio to a presentation and share via e-mail or social media.

As we said before, if a student is getting growth messages at school and fixed messages at home, it can become confusing. Share growth mindset with your parents, and get them on board. Who knows? You may convert a few fixed-mindset parents in the process!

STRATEGIES FOR BUILDING RELATIONSHIPS WITH COLLEAGUES

When Dan started his first teaching job at a local high school, he was told that the teachers all ate together at lunchtime in the cafeteria with the students. It wasn't mandatory, but it was kind of an unspoken rule. It would be weird if he opted out. At first, Dan says he felt annoyed because, as a first-year teacher, he fully anticipated spending his lunch breaks stuffing a sandwich in his mouth while hunched over the copy machine. But a funny thing happened. Dan quickly began to look forward to his lunches with colleagues. They chatted about teaching stuff sometimes, but mostly they made small talk about what was happening in their lives outside the school. This togetherness created a camaraderie with his colleagues that Dan realized he really missed when he went to work at another school with no such lunch obligation.

When teachers build strong relationships with their colleagues, it benefits the entire school culture. And just like with students, you can't share the growth mindset with colleagues without first having a solid foundational relationship.

Like students, other teachers need to know that you believe in their ability and competence as educators before they'll buy into your growth-mindset messages.

Here are some ways to improve relationships with and learn from colleagues in your school:

Mentoring. You're always in the position to be mentored. No matter what, there's someone in your building who has something of value to share with you. Seek out that person! Don't turn down opportunities to mentor others, either. It's a chance to share and reflect on your best teaching practices, and you'll probably learn a thing or two in the process, as well.

PLC groups. Form or join a professional learning community. If you're already involved with a PLC, try to take a more active role. Here you'll have many opportunities to learn from and collaborate with other teachers, and share your learning about growth mindset.

Committees. Get involved! Ask to join a committee you're passionate about. You'll get the opportunity to talk to teachers with whom you have this passion in common.

PBL planning. Plan project-based learning units together as a grade-level team or vertically and across the curriculum. PBL will allow your students to work on collaborative skills during a lengthy project, and it'll give teachers a chance to collaborate, as well.

Cooperative teaching. Co-teach a classroom with another teacher. Strive to collaborate, communicate, and learn from the co-teacher. This could be arranged as a long-term situation or as a short-term collaboration between classes.

Book clubs. Choose an education-themed book each quarter for teachers to read, then meet and discuss thoughts and feelings on the book. This strategy is sure to spark interesting conversation, forge connections, and inspire new ideas.

Build interpersonal relationships. Communication between teachers doesn't have to be all "shop talk." Make sure to have cordial conversations with colleagues about their personal lives. Bonding over a shared love of a band or baseball team or inquiries about family or hobbies can go a long way in building a friendly rapport.

Interest inventories. At the beginning of the year, distribute interest inventories to teachers, and publish the results. Through common interests, teachers who wouldn't normally work together may forge relationships with one another, creating a more cohesive school culture.

***

Now write down three ways to connect and build relationships with colleagues. For example: This year, I will join the curriculum committee to spend time with other teachers passionate about curriculum and instruction.

1. ______________________________

____

____

2. ______________________________

____

____

3. ______________________________

____

____

WHY RELATIONSHIPS MATTER

Why are we devoting an entire chapter to building relationships? Because relationships can make all the difference. Teachers in the fixed mindset will say that they don't have much to learn from students, parents, or colleagues. Teachers in the growth mindset, on the other hand, know other people are their greatest allies in being successful at work and life. The growth-mindset teacher values other people because other people can teach us a lot.

If you want to build a growth-oriented classroom and school culture, it's imperative that you spend time building relationships. What good is it to say that you believe in every student's potential to achieve through hard work and effort if your actions are telling a different story? Our monthly mantra is "I am a valued member of this learning community." Don't just tell people they are valued, go out of your way to make them feel they are valued, and believe the effort in relationship building will pay dividends in your personal and professional growth.

5

DECEMBER: WE LOVE A CHALLENGE!

If you aren't in over your head, how do you know how tall you are?

—T. S. Eliot

OBJECTIVES

- ✓ Teach students the difference between equity and equality.
- ✓ Develop strategies to challenge all students responsively and responsibly.
- ✓ Set and communicate high expectations of all students.

A FORMULA FOR GROWTH

In July 2012, a team from the Center for American Progress dove into student survey data collected in the biannual National Assessment of Educational Progress and was startled to discover a shocking number of American students who reported not being challenged enough in school.[45] Despite America's notorious reputation for testing its students to the point of exhaustion, an overwhelming number of our students were reporting classroom experiences lacking in challenging work. According to the survey data analyzed by researchers, here are some of the findings:

- 29 percent of American eighth graders and 37 percent of fourth graders describe their math work as often or always too easy.
- 57 percent of eighth graders believed history work was often or always too easy.
- 21 percent of American high school students said that their math work was often or always too easy; 55 percent of high schoolers said their history work was often or always too easy.

In other words, almost a third of American eighth graders surveyed were reporting a lack of challenge in school. Finding and relishing a challenge is one of the cornerstones of the growth mindset, so offering sufficiently challenging work is critical in developing a growth-oriented classroom. If perseverance, grit, and tenacity are the building blocks of a growth mindset, we must give our students opportunities to hone these qualities.

Dweck often emphasizes the value of challenging learning tasks. Writing in the *Educational Leadership* journal, she said, "It is crucial that no student be able to coast to success time after time; this experience can create the fixed-mindset belief that you are smart only if you can succeed without effort."[46]

Challenge is at the crux of the growth mindset; without it, students don't get the opportunities to take risks, learn to fail, and figure out how to pick themselves up again. This "sense of progress," as Dweck calls it, is central to developing growth mindsets. The slow trudge to mastery is a difficult but satisfying journey, so it is disheartening that so many American students report not getting the chance to walk this path of progress.

This month, we focus on challenging your students in ways that will develop their growth mindsets. We ask you to get creative in your lesson planning and curriculum design to make sure that every student in your classroom is sufficiently challenged. And we break down a formula we've developed that, in our experience, continually delivers results:

Nurturing Environment + Challenging Work + High Expectations = Growth

Last month we talked about the importance of creating a nurtured classroom, in which kids feel empowered to take learning risks. Let's break down each of the other two components of this formula: presenting your students with challenging, rigorous learning opportunities and setting high expectations for the progress and achievement of each student in the classroom.

OFFERING CHALLENGING WORK

We believe that all students need to be challenged with meaningful work. Not just gifted students. All students. All students in your class should believe that the work they're doing every day has a purpose, and that purpose should drive them to put forth the effort required to master it. They may not like the work, but the work must have meaning and value. It should be a priority to communicate the meaning and value to your students, and if you cannot articulate the purpose behind the lesson you're teaching, maybe you shouldn't be teaching it.

Here are some questions you can ask yourself as you plan a lesson to make sure it's sufficiently challenging for all your students:

- Are all students engaging in challenging work?
- Have I differentiated the material so all students feel sufficiently challenged?
- Are students encouraged to take a risk?
- How am I recognizing students for taking risks and overcoming challenges?
- What supports are available to help the student when he or she encounters an obstacle?
- Does the student see value in the process?
- What can I do to meet the learning goals of each student?

- How will I know if the students are engaged in challenging work? What will I look for?
- What resources are available? Do I need to seek additional resources?
- What are the intended outcomes? How will I determine if the student grasped the concept?
- What will I do if a student doesn't meet the outcomes?
- What choices will I offer students?
- How will I encourage wonder?
- How will I provide appropriate guided practice?
- Do I know the learning styles my students prefer?
- What support do I need to help the student grow?
- How will I personalize assignments and tasks?
- What can I do to show my students I am passionate about their learning?
- Have I established classroom expectations for working with partners and small groups effectively?
- Do my students know how to "coach" each other respectfully?
- Do I believe all students can learn?

As you lesson plan, ask yourself some or all of these questions. A clear picture will begin to emerge as to whether you've made an effort to challenge your students on an individual level. If all students have the exact same expectations, it's very likely that some of your students will encounter a developmentally inappropriate learning challenge. Differentiating your expectations means that you're being responsive to the students' needs, whatever they may be. You probably went to a school where all students in a class were handed the same worksheets and were expected to do them in the same way in the same amount of time. No longer is this considered a best practice, which is why it's essential that teachers (and students) understand the difference between equity and equality in education.

EQUITY VERSUS EQUALITY

When explaining equity and equality to our students, we have a go-to image that perfectly illustrates the concept. In this two-panel drawing, a toddler, a child, and an adult are all standing behind a tall fence. On the other side of the fence, a baseball game is being played, and our three people want to see what's going on in the game. In one panel, "equality" is illustrated by each of the three people getting a wood crate to stand on. In this depiction of equality, defined as "the quality of being equal," the adult, who was already able to see over the fence, is now boosted far above it with the help of his box. The child, with the aid of the box, can now see over the fence, as well. But the toddler, despite having a box to stand on, still cannot see over the fence to watch the game.

In the next panel, "equity," defined as "the quality of being fair," the adult no longer has a box, and can still see over the fence. The child keeps his one box, and can see over the fence to watch the game. The toddler now has two boxes, and can finally see over the fence to watch the game, as well. This is equity. Each person in the illustration[47] has been given what he needs to succeed, even though what each person needs is different.

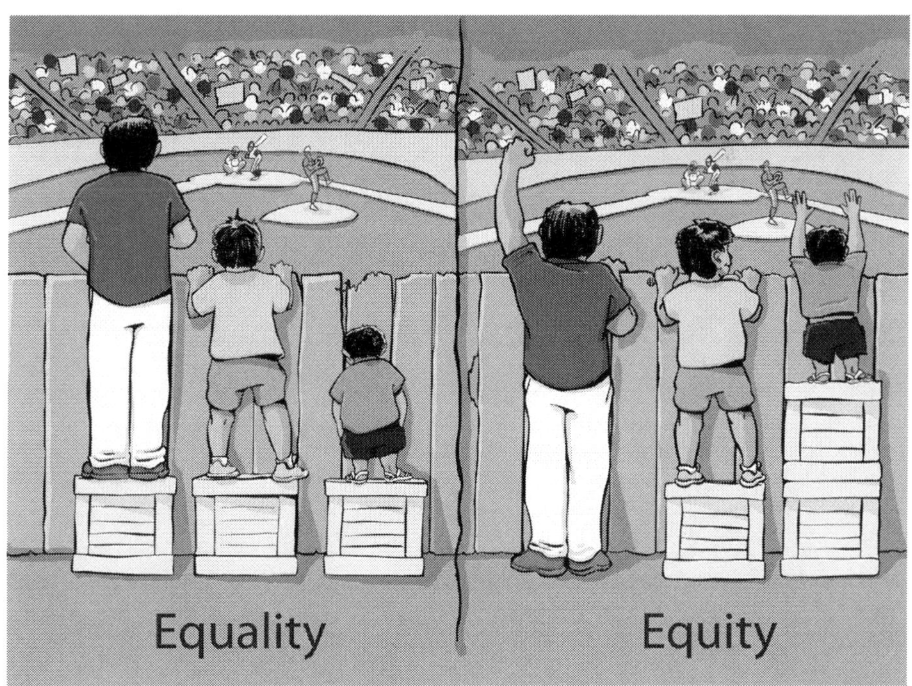

Equality is everyone getting one box (equal); equity is everyone getting to watch the game (fair). Let's review the definitions of equality and equity:

EQUALITY: The quality of being equal.

EQUITY: The quality of being fair.

Strive to create an environment of equity in your classroom, not equality. It's easy for teachers to confuse equity and equality, and fall into the false belief that fairness means all students are given the exact same tools, support, and opportunity. But the fact is, every student in your classroom will need different resources to succeed, and it's the teacher's job to find out what those resources are.

An effective way to determine what students need to succeed is to ask them directly. Opening a dialogue about equity is essential in a growth-mindset classroom. Some students may initially feel embarrassed to ask for extra resources or additional support, but once the class learns the difference between equality and equity, students may be more inclined to ask for what they need because now it has a simple name: equity. Here's a mini-lesson you can use to teach students the difference between equity and equality.

EQUITY VERSUS EQUALITY

LESSON PLAN

LEARNING OBJECTIVE

By the end of the lesson, students will be able to:

- explain the difference between equality and equity.
- demonstrate the difference between equality and equity.

RESOURCES AND MATERIALS

- Bowl of M&Ms
- Skittles or other small candy or snack
- Computer
- Projector
- Internet connection
- Equity versus equality statement chart
- Paper
- Drawing/writing utensils

METHOD

First, distribute one candy to each student. Ask, "How many M&Ms did I give you? Student answer: one. Say, "Yes, I gave each of you one M&M. This is called equality."

Define equality: "Equality is the quality of being equal. It means everyone is treated the same; in this case, we all have an equal amount of M&Ms."

Allow students to eat the candy.

Divide the class into two groups, and distribute note cards to each group. Instruct Group A students to write a statement about why a person would not need or want an M&M. For example: "I am allergic to chocolate." "I am really full from breakfast." Instruct Group B students to write a statement about why a person would need or want an M&M. For example: "I'm really hungry!" "My sweet tooth is craving chocolate." It's okay if the students get a bit silly with this!

Collect and redistribute the cards so all students have a card they did not write. Walk around the room with the bowl of M&Ms, and ask the students to accept or refuse your offer of M&Ms based on the statement on their note card. When a student refuses, move on to the next. When a student accepts the offer, ask the class to decide how many M&Ms to distribute based on the statement. For example, "I am really hungry," might result in an offer of five M&Ms, while "I love chocolate," may net only one or two.

After the M&Ms have been distributed say: *"This is equity. Equity means giving people what they need. Some of you didn't need or want the M&Ms, while others did. And, together, we used our judgment and passed out the M&Ms based on who needed them most. That is equity. Sometimes in class I will use my judgment to offer a student resources or support they need, like extra time to finish, an alternative assignment, or an audiobook instead of a textbook. That is equity in our classroom. Not everyone needs the same things. Let's look at an image that demonstrates this concept."*

Show students the equity versus equality image above. Point to the equality illustration and ask: *"When all three people get one box, what happens?"* Possible student responses: "One person cannot see"; "Someone who didn't need a box got one." Point to equity illustration and say: *"What happens when people get only the box or boxes they need?"* Possible student response: "Everyone can see." Say: *"Yes, that is equity. Everyone doesn't have an equal amount of boxes, but everyone does have what they need to succeed. Let's look at some examples of equity and equality. Help me decide if the situation represents equity or equality."* Engage students in a deeper discussion about why each situation represents equality or equity as you go through the items on the chart.

EQUITY OR EQUALITY?		
	EQUITY	EQUALITY
The teacher gives a student who didn't eat breakfast a granola bar.		
All students get a sticker as a reward for participating in a game.		
A student who has trouble seeing always gets a seat near the front of the class.		
Each student gets a turn feeding the class pet.		
The teacher asks which students need a pencil and gives a pencil to students who need one.		
Your brother needs to finish his homework and is allowed to stay up past bedtime.		
Both you and your sister get a Valentine from your neighbor.		
Your sister's shoes have a hole, so she gets a new pair.		

After reading several scenarios, ask students to draw or write one example of equity and one example of equality they have experienced.

CHECK FOR UNDERSTANDING

Check student drawings to determine whether they have correctly represented equity and equality. Continue to use the language "equity" and "equality" in class to reinforce the concept when appropriate.

DIFFERENTIATION AND CHALLENGE

Differentiation is an example of providing equity in education. Finding unique ways to differentiate material to meet the various needs of learners so all students feel sufficiently challenged is key in developing good curriculum that promotes a growth mindset. Differentiation typically happens in one of three areas: content, process, or product.

CONTENT: What the students are learning.

PROCESS: How the students are learning.

PRODUCT: How the students demonstrate learning.

There are always a few students who seem to master concepts and wrap up their work with seemingly no effort, so it's important that you build in extra challenge for these students through differentiation. Why? Let's take a look at an archetypal characterization of a student who isn't being sufficiently challenged at school:

This class is so boring! I don't even have to study and I can ace every test. I hate doing the assignments and homework my teacher gives me. I already know this stuff, but then I get graded off for spelling something wrong or not showing my work. Why should I have to explain how I know? I just know! Sometimes we do interesting things, but we don't get into it nearly as much as I want. I'm just going to get through this as fast as possible so I can read my book or play on the computer. Or maybe I just won't do it at all.

When students aren't sufficiently challenged, they become frustrated. Here are some strategies for differentiating the material in the different areas of content, process, and product for a child who needs more challenging work.

STRATEGY	DESCRIPTION	TYPE OF DIFFERENTIATION
PREASSESSMENTS	Determine where learning starts for your students. Assess their current knowledge. What do they already know? Offer lessons that stretch students far beyond their starting point.	CONTENT
VARIETY OF TEXT AND COMPLEXITY LEVELS	Provide access to a wide variety of materials. Provide extra materials for students who want to extend learning. Offer texts ranging in complexity.	CONTENT
LEARNING CONTRACT	Create an agreement with a student in which you mutually decide a developmentally appropriate course of learning.	CONTENT/PROCESS
FLEXIBLE PACING	Allow students to move through material at their own pace; avoid strict time limits.	CONTENT
HIGHER-ORDER THINKING	Use Bloom's taxonomy to develop activities that promote higher-order thinking; move away from words like understand and memorize and toward words like classify and construct.	PROCESS
PARTNER TALKS	Students discuss questions and ideas with a partner.	PROCESS
ALTERNATE ASSIGNMENTS	Offer students choice in their product. Instead of a traditional book report, students might choose to develop an app or board game based on the book, for example.	PRODUCT
MUST DOS AND MAY DOS	Offer students a prioritized list of tasks that must be done first (e.g., watch an instructional video), along with a list of valuable, but less important, tasks that may be done when the first tasks are finished (e.g., a coding activity). This way no one is ever left with nothing to do.	PRODUCT

On the flip side, there are students who may still be struggling to master a concept when the majority of the class is ready to move on. Here's an archetypal representation of how a struggling learner in need of differentiation may feel:

Why does everyone around me seem to get this stuff? I must be stupid. I feel like I'm always behind, and it takes me twice as long to get my work done as the smart kids. If I don't get what's going on now, I'll probably never get it. I hope the teacher doesn't call on me because I have no clue what he's talking about. He'll probably give us only fifteen minutes to finish the assignment, and I'll spend more time worried about the stupid clock than I will about finishing my assignment. This class is so frustrating, I might as well give up.

Providing support for struggling learners is key to promoting equity in the classroom. Forcing students to move away from a concept before they've mastered it is a good way to develop those "I stink at this!" attitudes that feed the fixed mindset. Consider working on a concept in chunks that present smaller, more manageable challenges on the way to mastering the overall concept or skill.

Here are some other ways to differentiate for struggling learners:

STRATEGY	DESCRIPTION	TYPE OF DIFFERENTIATION
LEVELED TEXTS	Offer texts at various complexity levels.	CONTENT
AUDIO/VIDEO	Offer different vehicles for delivering content, like videos, podcasts, tutorials, etc.	CONTENT
GRAPHIC ORGANIZERS	Offer an array of organizers for learning new information and organizing schema.	CONTENT
CHUNKING	Break down complex tasks into manageable sections or chunks.	PROCESS
MANIPULATIVES	Use hands-on manipulatives so students can physically interact with the learning.	PROCESS
JIGSAW LEARNING	Students work to complete assigned tasks within a group. Each member contributes to learning.	PROCESS
ASSIGNMENT OPTIONS	Allow students choice in how to demonstrate learning; students may write a poem, perform a skit, write a report, etc.	PRODUCT
VARIED RUBRICS	Avoid one-size-fits-all rubrics that do not account for differences in learning.	PRODUCT

All students approach learning from different places at different paces. You may notice the differentiation strategies in both tables are generally appropriate for both underchallenged and struggling students. The hallmark of a great differentiation strategy is flexibility. Teachers need to be able to adjust challenges on the fly. Differentiating is a way to honor differences in learning by using techniques that provide more equity in the content, processes, and products students are interacting with and creating in your class.

PERSONALIZED LEARNING AND CHALLENGE

Sir Ken Robinson, an education researcher, writer, and speaker, rose to international acclaim with his 2006 TED Talk, "Do Schools Kill Creativity?" which has been viewed almost forty million times. In 2015, Robinson published a book, *Creative Schools: The Grassroots Revolution That's Transforming Education*, outlining a plan to revolutionize what he characterizes as America's broken school system. In the book, Robinson writes about personalizing education as an antidote to the deeply impersonal "factory" model currently in use. "Education should enable young people to engage with the world within them as well as the world around them," he says.[48]

Whether or not you agree with Robinson about the state of American education, personalized learning is gaining traction as a teaching methodology that seeks to honor students' autonomy, learning styles, interests, and passions. Perhaps this is the greatest way to challenge and engage your students: tap into what students are passionate about on a personal level and weave it into an overarching curriculum meaningful to what they'll experience in the world. As personalized learning and student-led learning have become more popular in classrooms, teachers are experimenting with incorporating methods like 20% time, genius hour, passion projects, and inquiry-based learning as ways to engage students in interesting, challenging work by presenting them with learning opportunities directly linked to things about which they are passionate. It's also a way to allow students voice and choice in their own learning. Let's take a look at a few of these methods in more detail.

20% time. Provide students an opportunity to design their own learning with 20% time. 20% time comes from Google's company policy that allots 20% of employees' daily work time to projects of high interest to the employees. According to the theory, offering time to work on passion projects encourages innovation and creativity, which will spill over into other areas of work. For students, it also encourages in-depth learning and can motivate them to continue learning beyond the school day.

Passion projects. Students create an essential question that will drive their learning. They work through the process of determining what they already know and what they would like to learn, and then develop a plan of action to answer the question. Students are given the opportunity to direct their own research, design a learning process, reflect on challenges, and share their learning experiences.

Genius hour. Genius hour provides students an opportunity to design their learning based on their passions and interests by allotting one hour per week to individual pursuits. Students are encouraged to be innovative and are guided in applying their knowledge to solve problems and to ask additional questions that evolve from the process. Teachers facilitate the learning and coach students throughout the learning process.

Inquiry-based learning. Students are driven to learn based on questions they have about a given topic or concept. The teacher doesn't share what students should know or will learn, though the teacher launches a lesson by putting students in the driver's seat and encouraging them to learn based on their questions and the inquiry process. During inquiry-based learning, the teacher responds to students by asking additional questions, which may spark curiosity and investigation. Students are provided class time to make connections and critically think about solutions or outcomes.

ADVENTURES IN DIFFERENTIATION MRS. H'S JOURNAL

As I was preparing to introduce one-to-one correspondence using a large, colorful abacus on the first day of school with my kindergarten learners, I realized that I would have to dig deep to help a student who was far beyond the kindergarten math curriculum.

My first question to my new students was: Does anyone know what this tool is called or what we might use this for in kindergarten? I asked students to share their ideas with a partner. My next question was: How many beads do you think are on this abacus? The students had a variety of kindergartenish answers—from forty to a million. Then Jordan piped up and said, "There are exactly one hundred beads." I asked Jordan how he knew the answer, thinking that he may have counted by tens or was otherwise drawing from his schema.

"I know that there are ten beads on each row and there are ten rows. When you multiply ten times ten you get one hundred," said Jordan, matter-of-factly. Needless to say, this student was beyond learning how to count to one hundred using one-to-one correspondence. Based on an interest inventory I had requested all parents to complete prior to school, I knew Jordan had been an avid reader since the age of three and was deeply interested in the world around him. He was curious and intrinsically motivated to be the director of his own learning.

Later that day, I asked Jordan what he was hoping to learn in kindergarten. He thought for a moment and told me he really wanted to learn how to tell time. Perfect! We developed a plan of study to help him learn to tell time on an analog clock. This was a great starting point for Jordan, and it became vital in assisting him with other areas of study that were challenging to him.

Jordan could quickly grasp a concept when given a task with a high amount of structure and verbal logic, but was easily challenged and frustrated when the tasks were open-ended, requiring him to think critically or creatively. As bright as he was, Jordan could spend hours accomplishing very little toward a learning goal. He required a highly individualized instruction plan, as well as a lesson in building his capacity for a growth mindset. I had to ensure that he felt comfortable taking risks and to emphasize the effort and process of his learning. I asked Jordan's parents to provide him more opportunities to fail at home and to discuss his feelings surrounding failure. I also wanted them to talk to Jordan about expectations, the power of yet, and how he could problem solve or think critically about problems.

Jordan had a positive learning attitude, but he easily resorted to "I don't know" if he couldn't answer something quickly or if he thought he might be incorrect. He would also become very frustrated if he wasn't correct. I knew that I had to teach Jordan how to persevere, and to do that I needed a strong growth-oriented classroom. I had to let him know my classroom was a safe environment in which to tackle risks, make mistakes, and learn about himself.

I challenged Jordan by building his confidence in learning based on his strength in verbal cues through the use of a highly structured system of graphic organizers and time lines. Jordan was lost when I provided open-ended activities in which he developed the course of his learning or when the outcome of the learning wasn't clearly defined for him. For example, during composition journal writing, I would pose a question and expect students to write about the question by answering it with their own knowledge, ideas, and experiences, or by asking additional questions, describing how they would attempt to find the answer by inventing a solution, or simply by drawing a detailed illustration showcasing their thinking.

This helped Jordan to establish a sense of control. Together we were able to create a comfortable learning structure and foster his perseverance by moving forward rather than floating in a bubble of fear of not completing a problem correctly. Writing was a useful way to encourage and challenge his thinking. There was no right or wrong answer, only his thoughts and how he could support his thinking. Most important, it was a safe thinking environment in which all students shared their writing, gathered ideas from their peers, supported each other, and grew in their learning. We were a community of learners, all in a different place with our learning, but all working toward challenging ourselves to go above and beyond.

Inquiry-based learning about Jupiter was one of the first independent projects Jordan worked on in class. He was intrinsically motivated to learn about Jupiter. He had a strong interest in space exploration, and I used that interest as a platform to engage him in higher-level learning. I wanted him to learn to ask questions and seek out answers that would lead to even more questions. I wanted him to solve problems, to think critically, to try new solutions, to fail and resolve to try a new plan, to be innovative, to persevere, and to share with his peers what he learned and his path to learning it. Now you might be thinking this is a lot to ask of a five-year-old, but I can assure you, students will rise to the challenge in a safe learning environment. They will help each other on their learning journey, and they will become active learners and mindful problem solvers.

I helped Jordan build his creativity by encouraging him to design a board game that would help students practice multiplication. He knew several multiplication facts, but he learned strategies for those facts he didn't know.

In the process, he learned how to explain his thinking, design arrays, apply his knowledge toward solving division problems, and enhance his creative thinking by designing a fun and interactive game for his peers based on their interests.

Jordan surveyed the students in our class to find out what they liked in board games: dice or cards, points over movement on a board, two players or four players, and so forth. He took the information and began to plan, design, and build and rebuild his game. He even thought of additional ways to improve the game. He listened to the feedback of his peers and added their ideas.

By differentiating my approach to educating Jordan, he was able to concentrate on developing necessary skills like problem-solving strategies. He practiced perseverance by working through computer science tasks, learning how to play chess, solving logic puzzles, and engaging in cooperative learning tasks. These things were challenging for him, where the traditional curriculum was not. I believe that making the effort to meet Jordan's learning needs helped him to grow his mind, encouraged him to enjoy challenges, inspired him to work with others, and enhanced his growth mindset.

PERSONALIZED LEARNING IS VALUABLE LEARNING

We understand teachers have standards they're required to help their students master. But it's not imperative that you approach the teaching of those standards with a "one-size-fits-all" style that doesn't engage all your students. Sure, some concepts may lend themselves to whole-group instruction, but it doesn't have to be your default setting. Personalizing instruction gives educators the opportunity to challenge and engage students in a way that classical whole-group instruction does not. Start small by experimenting with an inquiry-based learning project in which the student decides what he or she wants to learn, and build from there. There are even classrooms in which every student learns according to his or her very own personalized learning plan.

Dweck agrees that personalized learning plans are a great way to offer challenging, meaningful work to students because individualized plans incorporate the students' interests, have a commitment from the student, and have a presentation component that provides an opportunity for students to transfer knowledge to other students.[49] There's great value in a teacher making an effort to personalize learning to the greatest degree possible, namely, the students often feel a greater degree of ownership over the work that compels them to invest themselves in its success.

SETTING HIGH EXPECTATIONS

Robert Rosenthal is a renowned researcher on the science of expectancy—how our expectations can influence outcomes. In the 1960s, Rosenthal made his graduate psychology students unwitting participants in one of his studies on expectancy.[50] His student researchers were given ordinary lab rats they were tasked with conditioning to run a maze. Some of the students were told that their rats had been specifically bred to be "maze bright"—genetically gifted when it came to running mazes. Another group was told that their rats were "maze dull"—or bred to have lower-than-average maze-running abilities. In truth, none of this was accurate: the rats were just, well, *rats*, so one might assume that they would all perform similarly at mastering the mazes.

But the results of the study showed the falsely labeled maze-bright rats performed significantly better at learning the mazes than their maze-dull counterparts. What could account for this discrepancy? Rosenthal believed that the information the student researchers were given concerning the dullness or brightness of their rats created certain expectations of outcome. Those expectations gave way to interactions that led to a self-fulfilling prophecy of sorts. The student researchers who believed that they were handling maze-bright rats reported being more satisfied with the performance of the rats. They also were more friendly and encouraging to the maze-bright rats, as well as less loud and more focused on them than the students with maze-dull rats. When the students believed that the rats would do well in the mazes, the rats acted accordingly. Rosenthal believed that it was the expectation of ability that influenced the researchers' relationship with the rats and paved the way for superior performance.

Writing about the results of his experiment in *American Scientist*, Rosenthal said, "If rats became brighter when expected to, then it should not be far-fetched to think that children could become brighter when expected to by their teachers."[51]

This theory led Rosenthal to try his experiment in a school, which resulted in his discovery of a phenomenon he termed the "Pygmalion Effect." In this experiment, Rosenthal gave kindergarten through fifth-grade students an intelligence test their teachers believed would indicate whether a student was primed for intellectual growth that year — these students were the "bloomers." Then experimenters shared the names of those students earmarked as "bloomers" with their teachers. In reality, the students whose names were shared were chosen at random with no regard to the results of the phony IQ test.

One year later, the 20 percent of students who had been designated as having exceptional potential for growth were performing much like the maze-bright rats. They were, on average, performing better than the students who didn't get the "bloomer" designation. Like the researchers in the rat experiment, the teachers set high expectations for the "bloomer" students and engaged in communication — both verbal and nonverbal — that conveyed those high standards. And what happened? The students rose to the challenge and met the high expectations.

Beverly Cantello, one of the teachers who participated in Rosenthal's study, told *Discover Magazine* in 2015 that even though she was offended when she first learned of her role in the study, it heavily influenced the rest of her teaching career.[52] She described subsequently writing more "sophisticated lesson plans" on Claude Monet and world geography, as well as becoming more acutely aware of the integral role her expectations played in her students' achievements. Later Rosenthal outlined four factors that explained why high expectations were fueling better performance.[53]

ROSENTHAL'S FOUR FACTORS	
CLIMATE	The teacher demonstrates behavior toward the student that's considered warm and familiar.
INPUT	The teacher invests more time and energy in those students for whom the teacher has higher expectations.
OUTPUT	The teacher calls on students for whom the teacher has high expectations, more often demonstrating confidence in the student to know the answer.
FEEDBACK	The teacher gives a higher quantity of responses with better quality feedback to the students for whom the teacher has higher expectations.

The problem with some of the factors Rosenthal identified as indicative of higher expectations is that many of those behaviors are subconscious ones.

An involuntary bristling, a frown, a pat on the back, a smile—these are things teachers, and all people, do without really thinking about it. These hundreds of nonverbal gestures a teacher makes every day can communicate feelings and attitudes toward students and have the potential to bolster or inhibit achievement. But, like Cantello describes, an awareness of how damaging low expectations are for students might be enough to help teachers be intentional about setting high expectations and believing in the potential of each student to achieve them. Those beliefs, on the part of the teacher, will perhaps manifest in physical cues and involuntary gestures that relay high expectations.

As with growth mindset, we have to believe that achievement is possible in order for it to work. Consider trying a few strategies in each of the four areas Rosenthal described.

ROSENTHAL'S FOUR FACTORS IN PRACTICE			
CLIMATE	INPUT	OUTPUT	FEEDBACK
Establish class norms so all students are familiar with the desired practices of the classroom, which has clearly defined procedures and codes of conduct.	Develop go-to strategies students can access. For example, in problem solving you may establish an "Ask three, then ask me" protocol to encourage peer feedback.	Allow students to coach one another to try new methods, research, review work, etc.	Offer YET feedback when a student struggles with a problem: "You haven't got it" versus "You haven't got it yet."
Use positive, appropriate physical reinforcement (hugs, high fives, fist bumps, secret handshakes).	Give students clear examples of great work, so they know what you expect of them.	Display work from students that shows improvement or hard work, not perfection.	Avoid unhelpful feedback like "good job" or "nice work." Always avoid negative generalizations like "You're a bad kid."
Smile at and interact warmly with all students; avoid sighing, glaring, rolling eyes at all times.	Involve all students in developing rubrics. Make sure all students are very clear about what is expected.	Call on all students when asking questions, and give them equal time to answer.	Be specific about what you liked about the student work.

Offer students autonomy over tasks.	Use the I Do, We Do, You Do (or gradual release of responsibility) method; this includes modeling through direct instruction and guided practice as you work through the learning process together.	Allow students to engage in independent practice.	Provide effort-oriented, specific feedback as the student works through learning tasks and independent practice.
Show an interest in the personal lives of all students; this communicates respect. Inquire and connect to their backgrounds. Ensure student diversity is represented in the books, music, poetry, and current event topics utilized in class.	Provide equity in time, attention, support, and resources; ensure that each student can access the tools he or she needs to succeed.	Ask all students for ideas and opinions; find positive ways to compel students to contribute.	When returning and discussing finished student work, provide explicit instruction on what the student can do to improve the work.
Make strong eye contact with all students; teachers tend to make less eye contact with students of whom they have lower expectations.	Check in on all students as they're engaging in work to make sure they're on the right track.	Give all students opportunities to practice skills.	Always give opportunities for students to address feedback and resubmit work.
Make efforts to be in physical proximity to all students; teachers may tend to sit high-expectation students in the front of the room. Avoid this practice.	Be available equally to all students to answer questions, provide guidance, etc.	Give all students equal opportunities for extra credit, projects, and classroom jobs and tasks.	Always communicate your belief in the potential of the student to succeed; reinforce achievement and positive performance with appropriate praise.

There's no doubt about it, a mountain of research tells us students pick up on the verbal and nonverbal cues we send to them that communicate our expectations. Before, we learned that explicitly telling students about growth mindset can increase their achievement, and research has found that sharing your high expectations can also fortify their achievement.

David Yeager, University of Texas, and Geoffrey Cohen, Stanford University, both collaborators with Dweck, conducted a study published in the *Journal of Experimental Psychology: General.* As part of the study, seventh-grade students turned in a rough draft of an essay they'd written about a personal hero. Teachers graded the essays normally, giving feedback on grammatical errors, word usage, and clarity, along with any encouragements they would normally offer. At random, the researchers attached one of two sticky notes on each student's essay. One offered a "wise feedback" message that read: "I'm giving you these comments because I have very high expectations and I know that you can reach them." The "control note" contained a less-inspired message: "I'm giving you these comments so that you'll have feedback on your paper." The students were then given an opportunity to resubmit the paper.

The results indicated that students were much more likely to take advantage of fixing and resubmitting the essay when they were given the wise message. African-American students who received the message with high expectations were a shocking 60 percent more likely to resubmit the essay than their counterparts who did not receive an improvement message. The researchers concluded that, especially where traditionally underserved students were concerned, students could only fully benefit from the teacher's feedback when it also included messages about the teacher's belief in the student's ability to meet high standards. Without the boost of the psychological feedback ("I have very high expectations and I know you can reach them"), the feedback on the work itself was far less effective in helping students improve academic performance.

The combination of hard work and high expectations can create the perfect conditions for facilitating growth mindset, but only if struggle in the face of challenge is met with encouragement on the part of the teacher. The right kind of feedback and praise can be a powerful motivator for reinforcing the growth mindset and the value of effort and perseverance, but the wrong kind of praise and feedback can send your students spiraling into their fixed mindsets.

6

JANUARY: FEEDBACK IS A GIFT—ACCEPT IT

I think it's very important to have a feedback loop, where you're constantly thinking about what you've done and how you could be doing better.

—Elon Musk

OBJECTIVES

✓ Distinguish between person praise and process praise.

✓ Develop strategies for giving effective feedback.

✓ Teach students how to use effective feedback when conferencing with peers.

THE PITFALLS OF PRAISE

In a 2007 article by Po Bronson in *New York Magazine*, "How Not to Talk to Your Kid,"[54] Carol Dweck recounted an experiment she conducted with four hundred fifth-grade students from New York schools. Here's how the experiment worked: One of Dweck's research assistants would first present a fifth grader with a test featuring an easy-to-solve series of puzzles. When the puzzles were completed, the researcher gave each student one of the following two lines of praise:

"You must be smart at this."

or

"You must have worked really hard."

The students then had the opportunity to choose the test they wanted to take for the second round: an easy test like the first one or a much more difficult test from which, the researchers said, the student would learn a lot. Interestingly, the majority of students who were praised for being smart opted to take the easy test, while over 90 percent of the students praised for their effort chose the difficult test.

Dweck theorized that the students praised for being smart were only doing what they had come to believe was expected of them by teachers, parents, and, now, the researchers: to look smart at all costs. Dweck and her colleagues ran the experiment again. The students were first given a very easy test, but this time the choice was removed, and all the students had to take a second test that was much more difficult than the first. In fact, the researchers knew all the students would fail. Every single student did fail the difficult test, but those who had been praised for their effort after the first test chalked up their dismal results to lack of focus. The researchers noted that these children "got very involved [in the test], willing to try every solution to the puzzles."

The other children—those praised for their smarts—believed their lack of success was directly linked to their intelligence. After administering the difficult test, Dweck and her colleagues presented the students with one more test—another easy one this time—suspecting that the experience with the difficult test might affect performance. Sure enough, the students who were praised for their effort significantly improved their scores from the first easy test to the second. On the other hand, students who were praised for their smarts after the first test did about 20 percent worse on the second easy test. What happened? It seemed that when the students bombed the impossible test and didn't live up to the researcher's initial assessment of their intelligence, very quickly their self-confidence crumbled.

It was in the context of these simple experiments that Dweck began to formulate the idea of the fixed and growth mindsets. Dweck saw when students were praised for being smart, they wanted to hang on to that praise; they became less likely to take on risks and challenges so as not to jeopardize the "smart" label that had been bestowed on them. In essence, the students moved into their fixed mindsets for self-preservation — to avoid making mistakes and possibly contradicting the initial assessment of their intelligence. Conversely, the students praised for their effort had no such insecurities. They were able to exist comfortably in their growth mindsets where making mistakes is just a consequence of working hard and trying new things.

A BETTER WAY TO PRAISE

Our first objective for the month is to teach you the difference between person praise and process praise. Person praise focuses on a student's personal traits and qualities, like intelligence. "You're so smart" is a commonly heard example of person praise. The problem with this kind of praise is that it sends the message that students succeeded because of some inherent, inborn quality they possess, not the effort they put into the task. Process praise, which acknowledges effort, strategies, or actions that contributed to the success of a task, sounds more like this: "You worked really hard at that," sending the message that the amount of effort put into the task led to success.

PERSON PRAISE	PROCESS PRAISE
You're a natural at math.	These problems didn't give you much of a challenge. Let's move on to something that will really stretch your brain!
You're so smart.	I like how you used different strategies to figure out these problems.
You're such a good boy.	I appreciate that you cleaned up the art center without being asked.
What a brilliant artist!	Your effort in learning to paint is apparent in your picture.
You're a born writer.	Your writing shows that you understand the value of word choice.

The same idea can be applied to constructive critique, as well. Person critique is feedback that blames a failure or setback on a quality of the person: "You're not smart at math." Process critique focuses on the effort, or lack thereof, put into the task: "That strategy didn't work for you. What else could you try?"

PERSON CRITIQUE	PROCESS CRITIQUE
You really messed this up.	This didn't seem to work out for you. How could you approach this problem differently?
You did your best, but it's just not good enough.	You didn't meet your goal, but what did you learn?
Maybe piano just isn't your thing.	Keep practicing. Every day you get closer to mastering this.
You're such a naughty boy.	You made a bad choice. What will you do differently in the future?

See the difference? Because person praise or critique is directly tied to a student's intelligence or some other personal quality, it can make him or her feel insecure about tackling challenges and potentially making mistakes in the future. Better safe than stupid, right? But when the teacher ties success or failure to effort, strategy, or action, the child is not evaluated globally but just on this one thing—right here and right now. In this moment, unrelated to intrinsic qualities and personal traits, the student can better understand the connection between effort and achievement. In this moment, it has nothing to do with being smart or stupid. In this moment, it has everything to do with perseverance and the process of learning.

Dweck says that person praise, which attaches success to some trait or quality of the person, is fine when the person succeeds at the task.[55] But what about when students inevitably hit a setback? If they believe their success is attributed to personal traits, then those same personal traits must also be responsible for failure. Most people don't like to feel like rotten failures, so, the theory goes, the person will avoid challenging activities in the future to maintain their self-esteem. A student who is praised for intelligence and perfection, in other words, will shy away from learning tasks that don't demonstrate those two qualities. However, when the praise is attached to a process—an altogether separate entity from the person—the person's willingness to tackle new challenges and show resiliency in the face of mistakes and setbacks is not compromised by crippled self-efficacy.

Another trap that teachers can fall into is offering nonspecific praise. You know the kind of praise we're talking about: those short, laudatory phrases often featured in glittery script on stickers, like "You're Awesome!" and "Great!" Even phrases like "Well done!" and "Good work!," while technically being process-oriented praise, are vague and don't provide much information to the student.

One article published on the popular teaching blog *Cult of Pedagogy* called this type of praise "Paula Praise,"[56] in reference to Paula Abdul's judging technique on the singing reality competition *American Idol*. Both Paula and Simon Cowell left a lot to be desired where feedback is concerned. Most people remember Simon's nasty zingers, like "You sound like a cat in a vacuum cleaner" or "You sounded like Cher after she's been to the dentist." Simon's feedback often lacked compassion and helpfulness, but never specificity. Paula's praise, on the other hand, was totally forgettable. Lots of "Great job!" and "Amazing!" but very little substance. You could always count on Paula to give a vague compliment, but, in the same way, you couldn't really count on Paula at all.

The problem with this kind of nonspecific feedback is the lack of context; it doesn't address what the student has done well. If you're going to put a sticker proclaiming "Good Job!" on a piece of student work, make sure it's accompanied by some effective feedback in the form of a short note or verbal comment describing what exactly was good about the work in terms of process.

VAGUE PRAISE	SPECIFIC PRAISE
You're awesome!	You're putting awesome effort in on this fractions assignment.
Good work!	Good work writing a detailed essay.
Well done!	Well done on your dance recital. I can see that you've practiced a lot.
Great!	Great strategy; that took some creative problem solving.

The teacher isn't the only one in a classroom who delivers praise and feedback. Students are often tasked with giving each other praise and feedback, and routinely critique their own performance. Here are some common examples of person praise and feedback you may overhear from your students, along with ideas on how to reframe those comments into process praise and feedback.

PERSON PRAISE/ FEEDBACK	PROCESS PRAISE/FEEDBACK
I don't understand long division.	You don't understand long division, yet!
Tina is the smartest kid in the class.	Tina did well on this exam. You should ask her how she studied.
This is too hard for me.	Hard is good! It means you're learning.

TEACHER FEEDBACK STEMS

Using feedback stems is a simple way to ensure that you're providing useful process-oriented feedback on student work.

How to use this resource: make copies of feedback stems, cut them into strips, finish the stem by writing specific process feedback, and attach to student work.

I noticed how . . .
Look at how much progress you've made on . . .
I see a difference in this work compared with . . .
I admire how hard you have worked on . . .
I can see you really enjoyed learning . . .
Could it make a difference if you . . .
Have you considered trying a different strategy to . . .
You're on the right track here, and might consider . . .

Another great way to help students reap the benefits of process praise and critique is to actively teach them how to praise and offer feedback to one another. Let's take a look at what student-delivered praise and critique looks like in Mrs. H's classroom.

PEER FEEDBACK THAT WORKS
MRS. H'S JOURNAL

In my kindergarten classroom, students are given time daily to work on developing writing skills and constructing sentences. Prewriters begin with illustrating their ideas and learning how to add details to their drawings. I have found giving step-by-step directions through I Draw, You Draw tasks helps students build their skill set for illustrating, provides them with strategies for design, and gives me an authentic way to illuminate student effort through modeling process praise.

During guided drawing time, I tell students how important it is to have a great learning attitude (growth mindset). I remind them how tackling a new skill can be challenging, and through our struggles, we are stretching our mind. As students practice developing their drawings, I walk around the room and share process praise and critiques with students. Personalizing feedback, asking questions, offering strategies, and engaging with students in their struggles help me establish a growth-oriented classroom environment. Students hear me say things like "Keep working hard; you're not quite there, yet," or "Have you tried using a different strategy, you might ask Tommy how he worked through his illustration," or "Wow, I can see you are applying what you learned about sketching houses to your drawing," or "I really like how much detail Selena has added to her illustration. I can tell she really worked hard to go above and beyond."

Students also share their writing and illustrations with a partner or in small groups, actively seeking critiques to improve their writing. Prior to allowing students to share their work, I present mini-lessons on specific skills and strategies regarding how students can coach their peers in revising their writing by giving helpful feedback.

When students meet with their classmates, they are directed to give process praise about something their partner has done well. As the students offer one another process praise, one might hear them saying things like "I really like how you added those details to your illustration to show that it's summer," or "You really worked hard to include our sight words in your sentence," or "Great work on remembering to capitalize the first letter of your sentence."

Students are then encouraged to coach their partner by offering revision feedback using process critiques. Peer coaching sounds something like this: "I think you're still working on learning to spell our new sight word; do you want to do the actions for the word?" or "How can you add more detail to your picture?" Students are explicitly taught how to use process critique to coach their partner in revisions. Offering students sentence stems and immediate feedback in their jobs, as peer coaches, helps them to develop these skills.

Learning to give effective praise and critique takes practice. Equipping my students with these tools has helped us establish a growth-oriented classroom environment. Students are willing to take on challenging tasks, take risks, and accept assistance from their peers. Daily, we work together to help each other grow as a community of learners by using effective feedback and thinking about ways we can improve.

STUDENT FEEDBACK STEMS

Feedback stems can also be useful in the peer evaluation process. These stems help students develop valuable process-oriented feedback to offer other students.

How to use this resource: make copies of feedback stems, cut them into strips, finish the stem by writing specific process feedback, attach to student work.

One awesome thing about your work is . . .
I really like the way you . . .
One thing that helps me is . . .
This could improve if . . .
My favorite part of this was . . .
I noticed that . . .

Changing the way you praise isn't going to be easy. It'll take dedicated mindfulness to develop process praise as a habit. More than once you'll catch yourself about to deliver some person praise and be forced to switch it up on the fly: "You're so smart . . . ly persevering through this challenge because you're a hard worker!" Yikes. Old habits die hard sometimes. But there's good news! The more you practice, the easier it will become. (Did you catch that process praise?)

REPHRASE THE PRAISE
MS. B'S JOURNAL

Once I learned about the growth mindset, I began to see it in action everywhere. One of my favorite places to take my children is the Mulvane ArtLab on the campus of Washburn University in Topeka, Kansas. Underneath the university's art gallery, the ArtLab is a colorful basement room filled with endless art supplies, Lego bricks galore, and kid-friendly works of art.

During one visit, my daughter, who had just turned three, was diligently working on a watercolor painting. A staff member of the ArtLab walked past our table, and my daughter proudly held up her drawing and asked the woman, "Do you like what I made?" Without skipping a beat, the staffer replied, "The question is, do ***you*** *like what you made?" My daughter was quiet for a moment as she processed the redirection, and then excitedly launched into an explanation about the colors she chose and the various aspects of her drawing.*

To me, this exchange reinforced what I already believed about the power of growth mindset: constructive feedback and praise opens the mind. With one question, this woman turned my daughter from an insecure toddler in search of validation into a delighted, engaged child confidently describing the thought and effort that went into her painting. Reframing my daughter's question turned a plea for praise into an exercise in critical thinking, completely changing the dynamic of the conversation. I found myself still pondering the exchange days later, thinking how I wouldn't have remembered it at all if the woman had said something dismissive like "Oh, very pretty!" and walked away.

Before I learned about the mindsets, I would not have recognized the ArtLab interaction for what it was: a generous opportunity for reflection and growth. I'm embarrassed to say, I might have even considered the woman rude for refusing to compliment my toddler's artwork! But because I know the value of cultivating a growth mindset in early childhood, I was grateful to this woman. Moreover, I hope for more adults in my children's lives who go out of their way to help them improve instead of dismissing them with trumped-up praise. My experience at the ArtLab with my daughter proved to me even our very youngest learners are capable of reacting to process praise and constructive feedback with critical thinking and thoughtful reflection.

THE LONG-TERM BENEFITS OF PROCESS PRAISE

In the course of early childhood development, babies, toddlers, and preschoolers can be significantly affected by the kind of praise they receive. Brain synapses are forming faster in early childhood than they will during any other period in life, which means kids are making connections and developing mindsets and habits they'll carry with them far into the future.

Researchers in Chicago followed fifty-three toddlers in their home environments, visiting every four months beginning shortly after the children's first birthdays.[57] During the visits, field researchers videotaped typical interactions between the parents and children for ninety minutes. At the end of the research period, roughly two years later, the videotapes were transcribed, and the praise parents offered their children in their daily interactions was categorized as process praise, person praise, or "other" praise. Other praise included nonspecific positive remarks like "Wow!" or "Nice picture!" that did not clearly fall into the process or person praise categories.

The researchers then visited the children some five years later when they were in second and third grades and administered questionnaires to determine their mindset and motivation. The results were clear: children of parents who offered more process praise than person praise demonstrated positive attitudes toward taking on new challenges and displayed more characteristics of growth mindset.

BETTER THAN PRAISE

We know the kind of praise we offer children can encourage fixed and growth mindsets, so it's important to be mindful of whether you're offering person praise or process praise. But according to Dweck, most parents and teachers are overpraising, anyway. A superior method of developing growth mindsets isn't offering process praise after the fact but interacting with the child as he or she works through a task. Dweck says that whenever you can replace praise with getting involved, do it. "Appreciate it. Ask questions. If we see that a child is using interesting strategies we can ask about them. Talk to them about their thought processes, how they learn from mistakes."[58]

7

FEBRUARY: A GOAL WITHOUT A PLAN IS JUST A WISH

Every worthwhile accomplishment, big or little, has its stages of drudgery and triumph: a beginning, a struggle, and a victory.

—Mahatma Gandhi

OBJECTIVES

- ✓ Understand how the personal quality of grit influences mastery.
- ✓ Guide students to research real-world examples of grit.
- ✓ Distinguish between performance goals and learning goals.
- ✓ Help students develop performance goals and learning goals.

THE MAGIC OF MINDSET

Aubrey Steinbrink is a sixth-grade language arts teacher at Spring Garden Elementary in the Dallas/Fort Worth area. When she stumbled on the concept of growth mindset, she knew immediately that it was going to be a game changer.

Steinbrink discovered growth mindset at the perfect time. The end of the 2012–2013 school year was fast approaching, and although her group of fourth graders—the grade level she taught at the time—had done well on their state assessments, she felt that they hadn't yet developed the ability to persevere, challenge themselves, or go beyond the status quo. In short, she felt as if she had let them down. But, as she said, "the Universe heard my concern and granted me another year with them as their fifth-grade teacher."[59]

Then she went about turning her classroom into a growth mindset zone. She took great care to organize her classroom to reflect the ethos of the growth mindset. She was purposeful with her decor choices. She created a plan for daily bell work that included songs, video clips, and picture books that echoed the growth-mindset messages she desperately wanted her students to absorb.

It wasn't long before her commitment to sharing the principles of the growth mindset with students started to manifest in meaningful change. She began to hear the growth-mindset messages she had been promoting inside her classroom in the hallways, cafeteria, and around the school. She saw more teamwork and collaboration and emphasis on the value of effort from her students all around the school. It seemed like the growth mindset was taking hold, but her biggest challenge was yet to come. Steinbrink recounts working with a group of students facing a difficult challenge: they had to retake a state exam they had previously failed before they would be allowed to move to the next grade.

Steinbrink said that these students believed "in their core" that they were stupid, and no amount of motivational pep talks was going to change that. So she began teaching them the science of neuroplasticity. She taught them the brain is like a muscle that can grow; she taught them about neurons and dendrite connections. The students watched video clips about the brain and even role-played making brain connections with yarn.

Sure enough, when the state scores came back a few weeks later, Steinbrink's formerly skeptical students realized not only could they pass the daunting test but they had managed to close some significant learning gaps in the process.

Steinbrink again moved with the same group of students to sixth grade, where she continues to incorporate growth mindset into her class every day. She begins the year by introducing the science of brain development, acquainting the students with how their brains learn and store new information. Steinbrink loves to show students video clips that illustrate growth mindset in action. She shows a clip, and then asks students to draw out the example of growth mindset and connect it to their own lives. She brings in team-building exercises and brain teasers, and is all about getting her students out of their comfort zones. Perhaps the most important part of her growth mindset training is helping students set goals.

Her students set daily goals, weekly goals, unit goals, and yearly goals. She's constantly challenging them to find new strategies to solve problems and strengthen their areas of weakness. Her students immerse themselves in reflecting on learning by examining their own formative assessment data and strategizing on how they can improve.

Steinbrink has had an overwhelmingly positive response from her students to her growth-mindset instruction. She'll often overhear students talking to one another with growth-mindset messages like "Give it a try" and "What could it hurt?" She sees the students forging connections with one another because together in her class they're exposing their vulnerabilities and trying new things. Steinbrink says that growth mindset has leveled the playing field for her students, in a sense, because they finally realize that intelligence is the result of a process, not a gift of genetics.

Steinbrink is the perfect example of how teachers can foster growth mindset in their students. She talks to them about trying to juggle teaching along with the extra work of earning her master's degree, she tells them stories about training hard for the 5Ks she loves to run, and she openly shares her personal struggles and successes to show students how a growth mindset sticks with and supports a person in every facet of life.

"I see my students setting goals, going further than they expected, and not letting setbacks finish them," said Steinbrink. "They are motivated, happy, and goal-oriented, and I am proud to be their teacher."[60]

Here are Ms. Steinbrink's favorite growth-mindset resources:

BOOKS

The Miraculous Journey of Edward Tulane, by Kate DiCamillo

Freak the Mighty, by Rodman Philbrick

Holes, by Louis Sachar

Maniac Magee, by Jerry Spinelli

The Iliad, by Homer (Paris and his brother)

Matilda, by Roald Dahl

Boy, by Roald Dahl

Marshfield Dreams: When I Was a Kid, by Ralph Fletcher

I Can't Accept Not Trying: Michael Jordan on the Pursuit of Excellence, by Michael Jordan

SONGS

Songs from *Rent*

"Imagine," by John Lennon

"Human," by Christina Perri

"Conqueror," by the cast of *Empire*

"Titanium," by Madilyn Bailey

"Try Everything," by Shakira

"Eyes Open," by Taylor Swift

"Fight Song," by Rachel Platten

"Lessons Learned," by Carrie Underwood

VIDEO CLIPS

"Failure" (Michael Jordan Nike commercial)

The Pursuit of Happyness (job interview clip)

Katy Perry: Part of Me ("Never Give Up" clip)

Grit: The Power of Passion and Perseverance (TED Talk by Angela Lee Duckworth)

"23 vs 29" (Michael Jordan Gatorade commercial)

Charlie Brown (any episode)

PICTURE BOOKS

Wilma Unlimited, by Kathleen Krull

Stand Tall, Molly Lou Melon, by Patty Lovell

Malala Yousafzai, by Karen Leggett Abouraya

The Invisible Boy, by Patrice Barton

Thank You, Mr. Falker, by Patricia Polacco

Oh, the Places You'll Go, by Dr. Seuss

Fox, by Margaret Wild and Ron Brooks

POETRY

"Never Enough," by Marina Lang

"Believe," by Tera Lee Jubinville

"Perseverance," by Pattra Shuwaswat

"Champion," by Justin Sorenson

"Courage," by Wish Belkin

GETTING GRITTY

As we learned from Ms. Steinbrink's story, goal setting is a powerful part of using the growth mindset to overcome challenges. Without a concrete idea of what you want and a vision of how you're going to get there, it's easy to slip back into the fixed mindset. The concept of grit is often interconnected with the incremental theory of growth mindset. First, let's take a look at what grit means, and then discuss goal-setting techniques to promote grit among your students.

In his book *Outliers*, Malcolm Gladwell writes about what he calls the "10,000 Hour Rule."[61] Gladwell cites a research study by the psychologist K. Anders Ericsson, who observed and compared violin students at the esteemed Academy of Music in Berlin, Germany, a school for music students who are considered the best of the best. Ericsson determined that the difference between students who had the potential to be world-class musicians and those who were, by comparison, just good was the amount of dedicated practice each student had completed. Ericsson calculated the best violinists had racked up ten thousand hours of practice by the age of twenty, while the "just good" students had clocked only eight thousand hours of practice. He then studied pianists with the same result. Ericsson just couldn't find evidence of the mythological "natural"—no student considered at the top of his or her class got there without putting in the ten thousand hours, and no student who had put in the ten thousand hours was considered just okay.

Angela Duckworth, a former middle school and high school math teacher, current professor of psychology at the University of Pennsylvania, and MacArthur Fellow, who has extensively researched the quality of grit—which she defines as "perseverance and passion for long-term goals"—concurs that the kind of deliberate practice Gladwell refers to with the "10,000 Hour Rule" is what leads to success. Duckworth recently published a paper with Ericsson, "Deliberate Practice Spells Success: Why Grittier Competitors Triumph at the National Spelling Bee,"[62] showing the amount of time students spent engaging in deliberate practice (e.g., time dedicated to individual, focused study and memorization, particularly on challenging aspects that go slightly beyond the scope of current ability) in preparation for the National Spelling Bee was the best indicator of success. The students rated this deliberate practice as less enjoyable than other styles of practice like mock bees and spelling with friends or parents, but nevertheless spent tremendous amounts of time engaged in it. Why? According to Duckworth, that's the grit.

In his book *Peak*, Ericsson argues that people have the ability to create their own potential through deliberate practice, and it's false to believe that we have predetermined potential for building skill or developing talent in certain areas.[63] According to Ericsson, people should stop believing that there's a ceiling on their potential, and instead view it as something that can be continually developed with learning and practice.

The concept of deliberate practice can be applied on a smaller scale than the 10,000 Hour Rule implies. Anyone can use the concept of dedicated practice to master smaller tasks like learning to juggle, writing a joke, or solving quadratic equations. In a recent interview on the *Freakonomics* podcast, Ericcson said that his graduate students at Florida State University do a boiled-down version of the ten thousand hours, instead spending ten hours engaged in deliberate practice trying to improve or master skills like typing or doing a handstand.[64]

American teachers probably are not in a position to personally train children to become masters in a given field, but what we're capable of is instilling in students the belief that with enough deliberate practice and dedication to a task, they can make incredible strides. This can be done on a micro level in the classroom, where we have daily opportunities to show students that deliberate practice and dedication to learning challenges can result in improvement.

SELLING GRIT

The idea that large amounts of deliberate practice, and not natural ability, leads to success is a valuable one for students developing a growth mindset. When students see how deliberate practice (and a healthy dose of failure) is almost always required to rise to the top of any field, the idea of growth mindset can better be cemented as a viable strategy for success. It shows, unequivocally, practice and effort, not genetics, lead to success.

Get kids thinking about how practice, training, and toil lead to great accomplishment by having them market "Grit" with a commercial featuring a famous person who has demonstrated grit. To begin, show students the Nike commercial "Failure" featuring Michael Jordan. (It's available to view on YouTube.) The commercial features a voice-over of Jordan saying:

"I've missed more than nine thousand shots in my career. I've lost more than three hundred games. Twenty-six times I've been trusted to take the game-winning shot, and missed. I've failed over and over and over again in my life, and that is why I succeed."

After watching the commercial, have students choose a subject and create a commercial illustrating the concept of perseverance and grit. First, have the students choose a famous person who is, or was at some point, at the top of their field. They may be tempted to choose fresh-faced actors starring in the Disney special du jour, but try to guide them to choose true masters in crafts. Then, have the students research that person and create a commercial for grit. The commercial will include things like how long the person has been working toward success, years of education he or she needed to complete, various setbacks along the way, and how the person continues to improve. Here are some well-known examples of "gritty" people—people who worked incredibly hard to get to the top of their fields.

- J. K. Rowling, author
- Michael Jordan, basketball player
- Kobe Bryant, basketball player
- Wolfgang Amadeus Mozart, composer
- Will Smith, actor
- Meryl Streep, actress
- Pablo Picasso, artist
- Walt Disney, Disney founder
- Henry Ford, Ford manufacturer
- Soichiro Honda, Honda manufacturer
- Bill Gates, Microsoft founder
- Harland David Sanders (a.k.a. "Colonel Sanders"), KFC founder
- Wright Brothers, aviation pioneers
- Stevie Wonder, singer
- Jim Carrey, actor
- Steven Spielberg, director
- Thomas Edison, inventor
- Oprah Winfrey, media mogul
- Abraham Lincoln, US president
- Bill Joy, computer scientist
- Tyler Perry, actor/director
- Tim Westergren, founder of Pandora

Students can create the video by using any number of devices, software, or apps. Some recommendations include Green Screen by Do Ink, iMovie, Stop Motion

Studio, Adobe Voice, iPhone/iPad camera, video camera, PicPlayPost, Magisto, Instagram Video (up to sixty seconds), and Andromedia Video Editor.

Some mistakenly believe that the people on this list are so naturally talented in their field that their path to success was an easy one. In fact, society likes to relish in the notion that some people are just born for greatness. But as students research and start uncovering the truth about how much sweat and toil, how many hours, how many failures go into creating a master, they'll understand the dogged dedication to a long-term goal required to achieve greatness. The message we want students to walk away with is that nothing really comes easy for anyone. Even if someone has a natural affinity in a given area, that person must dedicate thousands of hours to the pursuit to be considered truly great. We hope that this will leave students with a lasting sense that achievement is born of hard work, not mythical natural abilities that we're graced with at birth. Once they have this information, they can get down to the business of achieving goals with grit and perseverance.

PERFORMANCE GOALS VERSUS LEARNING GOALS

In *Drive: The Surprising Truth about What Motivates Us*, Daniel Pink writes about differences in the mindsets Dweck describes: "The two self-theories lead down two very different paths —one that heads toward mastery and one that doesn't. For instance, consider goals. Dweck says they come in two varieties—performance goals and learning goals. Getting an A in French class is a performance goal. Being able to speak French is a learning goal."[65]

What kinds of goals do the masters set for themselves? According to Dweck, people set both performance and learning goals for themselves, but only learning goals lead to mastery. Dweck conducted a study with junior high students, who were learning new material in a science class. At the beginning of the study, students created goals related to learning the new material. The researchers categorized the student-generated goals as either performance goals (a goal designed to make the student look smart and capable) or learning goals (a goal designed to help the student learn, regardless of performance).

Dweck noted in *Self-Theories: Their Role in Motivation, Personality, and Development*, that, in this study, the students who went the extra mile to engage in deep learning and challenging tasks were the students who had been identified as those who primarily set learning goals.[66]

Based on pretests, researchers determined that both categories of students, those considered performance-oriented and those considered learning-oriented, were approaching the new material with roughly the same amount of mathematical and numerical reasoning skill, and both groups performed similarly in demonstrating the material they learned in the unit. But when the students were asked to apply their new knowledge to novel problems—problems in which they must apply the material they've learned in new and different ways or think about the learning at the next level—the students who set the learning goals fared much better. The learning-oriented goal setters scored higher on novel problems and generated more work in solving novel problems, which included 50 percent more writing in regard to deeper-thinking questions.[67]

Researchers have also examined "classroom goal structures" to determine whether students are motivated toward learning goals or performance goals based on aspects of the classroom environment. The TARGET system, first constructed by the educational psychologist Carole Ames, identifies classroom dimensions that lend themselves to either performance-oriented or learning-oriented classroom goal structures. The TARGET system looks at six aspects, or dimensions, of classroom environment that lead to either performance-oriented or learning-oriented classroom goal structures: Task, Authority, Recognition, Grouping, Evaluation, and Time.[68] Look at characteristics of the different types of classrooms in the chart on the next page, and determine the goal structure of your classroom.

DIMENSION	DESCRIPTION	PERFORMANCE-ORIENTED CLASSROOMS	LEARNING-ORIENTED CLASSROOMS
TASK	Includes the type of learning tasks the students are assigned, and the rigor, engagement, and value inherent in the tasks.	Tasks are often considered too easy by the students and often include performance tasks (e.g., rote memorization and demonstration of math facts). Very little personalization of tasks; often not engaging to students.	Students work on challenging tasks that offer equity and variety in process and product, and are of high interest to the students. The students find meaning and value in the tasks assigned.
AUTHORITY	Includes the role of students as decision makers and directors of learning, and their role in classroom leadership tasks.	The teacher provides clear directives on tasks; there's little room for student input on tasks. Teacher is the leader of the class.	Learning is often student led; students are empowered to make decisions about learning tasks. Students are empowered to take on leadership in learning.
RECOGNITION	Includes how and why students receive recognition.	Students are incentivized and recognized for turning in flawless work, following rules, and finishing work efficiently. Taking risks and developing creative strategies are not encouraged.	Students are incentivized and recognized for demonstrating effort, improving skills, and accomplishing learning goals. Taking risks and developing creative strategies are encouraged.
GROUPING	Includes how students are grouped together in collaborative learning.	Homogeneous grouping strategies are used, including ability grouping; groups feature superficial collaborative efforts and underlying competitiveness between group members and among groups.	Heterogeneous grouping strategies that feature different learning styles, strategies, levels, and philosophies are used. Students are encouraged to engage in deep collaboration.
EVALUATION	Includes how the teacher assesses student work process and product and evaluation procedures in place.	No equity in assessment and evaluation; evaluation often done publicly with a focus on how students perform in relationship to one another.	Evaluation of students is varied, and done in a private fashion. Individual progress is often assessed with a focus on individual improvement and progress toward mastery.
TIME	Includes how a teacher plans class time and how time is used to complete tasks.	Time limits are strictly enforced, with little deviation from the original plan. Students are not given variation in time limits to complete tasks because of differences in learning place and pace. Quickness and efficiency is valued over mastery.	Students are encouraged to work at their own pace; schedule can be easily adapted to address gaps or allow for enrichment or remediation. Mastery is valued over quickness.

Does your class have more features of a performance-oriented classroom or a learning-oriented classroom? If teachers send the message that completeness and correctness are more valuable than learning, students will fall in line with that expectation. But, as Dweck showed with those junior high school students, the students who set learning goals focused on true mastery — a deep understanding from which students can draw conclusions, connect ideas, and build relationships to new skills and concepts — experience richer learning than students who focus on showing what they know. The type of goal structures inherent to your classroom will influence the personal goal orientation of your students.

In the performance-oriented classroom, the teacher ranks students according to their intelligence and encourages students to compare themselves to one another. The teacher focuses on a few "smart" students and doesn't make efforts to personalize learning to increase engagement or differentiate learning to accommodate different learning styles. In the learning-oriented classroom the teacher values mistakes as learning tools and values effort in a task over completeness of a task. In a performance-oriented classroom, equality is a virtue (same task, same amount of time, same product, same expectations); in a learning-oriented classroom, equity is a virtue (creativity and personalization of tasks, flexible time structures, accommodation of different learning styles, equitable treatment of students).

In a review of over one hundred studies on student motivation, Chris Watkins of the University of London reported that the meta-analysis suggests that while both performance and learning orientation drive student motivation and both are present in high-achieving students, the students who focused on performance did "less well academically, thought less critically, and had a harder time overcoming failure."[69]

Both the classroom environment and school culture can have a significant impact on students' goal orientation, and their goal orientation has a significant impact in their level of learning. A growth-mindset classroom is one that features the learning-oriented dimensions outlined in the TARGET framework. The masters who have put in ten thousand hours aren't working toward performance goals; they're working toward learning goals. Learning-oriented goals help students develop grit and dedication to learning over time, as opposed to performance-oriented goals, which are more about proving intelligence or ability on isolated tasks.

In the course of their learning, students will inevitably set both performance and learning goals for themselves, but it's important that they're able to distinguish between the two types of goals and understand that one goal will assist them in short-term comprehension and performance, and the other will lead them down a path of true mastery.

EXPLORING PERFORMANCE GOALS WITH STUDENTS

LESSON PLAN

LEARNING OBJECTIVE

By the end of the lesson, students will be able to:

- distinguish between learning goals and performance goals.
- write a learning goal and a performance goal.

RESOURCES AND MATERIALS

- Note cards
- Chart paper
- Whiteboard
- Markers

METHOD

Distribute blank note cards to students and ask them to define "goals" in their own words. Have all students share definitions with a partner and come up with a group definition encompassing both ideas. Ask partners to share definition and record key words and phrases on a whiteboard or chart

Say: "There are two main types of goals that people set: performance goals and learning goals." Define performance goals and learning goals for the students.

PERFORMANCE GOAL: A goal that focuses on demonstrating tasks, content knowledge, skills or abilities, and often how the acquired skill or task will be judged in comparison to others.

LEARNING GOAL: A goal that focuses on overall learning, particularly how mastery of a skill or concept will develop understanding and apply to subsequent learning and challenges.

Referring back to the chart, have the students determine what words and phrases from their definitions apply to learning-oriented goals (circle in green) and what words apply to performance-oriented goals (circle in red). Present the chart with the following examples, and have students categorize examples as either learning goals or performance goals.

	LEARNING GOAL	PERFORMANCE GOAL
I will get an A on my math final.		X
I will learn how to speak Spanish.	X	
I will score three goals in the soccer game.		X
I will learn how to play chess.	X	
I will earn an "exemplary" on my state assessment exam.		X
I will learn to apply the scientific process in my experimentation.	X	

Say: "Notice how the learning goals often focus on what the student will learn, while the performance goals focus on what the student will do or show. Research tells us that while both types of goals help students achieve in school, learning goals lead them to greater understanding and enhance their ability to apply what they've learned in new and interesting ways in future challenges. Think of it this way: performance goals will help you make a short-term achievement, but learning goals will help you define a path for long-term learning and success. Let's use the SMART goal-writing framework to write a sample performance goal and learning goal."

Using the SMART framework, have students write one performance goal and one learning goal. Once the goals have been written, create small groups to read and discuss the goals. Have students offer feedback to adjust goals to fit the learning and performance categories.

CHECK FOR UNDERSTANDING

Check student goals for evidence of understanding of performance goals and learning goals. Have students keep the goals to revisit and reflect on progress.

THE STRUGGLE

Mahatma Gandhi said that every worthwhile accomplishment has "a beginning, a struggle, and a victory." Students begin on a path of accomplishment with a well-defined goal, and in the pursuit of that goal, will be encouraged to show qualities of determination and grit. But willingness to face a challenge isn't the same as having the tools to overcome them. The next chapter, which addresses coaching through setbacks, will provide teachers with coaching strategies designed to teach students techniques for overcoming obstacles, failures, and setbacks in the pursuit of goals.

8

MARCH: MISTAKES ARE OPPORTUNITIES FOR LEARNING

How often I found where I should be going only by setting out for somewhere else.

— R. Buckminster Fuller

OBJECTIVES

✓ Learn how to coach students through mistakes.

✓ Develop mistake-friendly teaching strategies.

THE GENIUS MYTH

In American culture, Albert Einstein's name has become synonymous with "genius." If you've witnessed someone solve a difficult puzzle or problem, you might have even said, "Way to go, Einstein!" But here's the thing: Albert Einstein was often quick to refute claims of his own superintelligence. He's quoted as saying things like:

"I have no special talent. I am only passionately curious."

"It's not that I'm so smart, it's just that I stay with problems longer."

As a young child, Einstein's parents consulted a doctor because he was so late to begin speaking. He was also a late reader. He was forced to take his college entrance exams a second time after having failed the first.[70] Certainly, Einstein may have been born with some natural mental acuity where math and problem solving are concerned, but even he would have told you it wasn't his natural intelligence that propelled him to the greatest discoveries in the field of physics, it was his unceasing determination—what we call his growth mindset. When faced with failure, he tried again and again. Here are some snippets of Einstein's thoughts on failure:

"Failure is success in progress."

"Anyone who has never made a mistake has never tried anything new."

"The only sure way to avoid making mistakes is to have no new ideas."

Our cultural value of genius actually stands in stark contrast to the way our most notable genius, Einstein, lived his life, often eschewing his own intelligence and celebrating failure and mistakes as learning opportunities. When Einstein died, his brain was preserved for future research,[71] and while scientists did note some atypical distinctions in Einstein's brain, like dense neurons and a highly developed region linked to musical ability, both nature and nurture likely played a role in his intellectual success. The anthropologist Dean Falk says that while the inherent nature of Einstein's unusual brain may have been partly responsible for his impressive accomplishments, so were environmental factors. Einstein cultivated a reputation for doggedness in his learning and persistence through setbacks and challenges. He also appeared on the physics scene at a time when the relatively new field was ripe for discovery.

"He had the right brain in the right place at the right time," said Falk.[72]

Would Einstein's parents have taken odds on their son — who was slow to speak and considered "dull-witted" by his teachers — becoming one of the most brilliant, celebrated scientists the world has ever known? Actually, they probably would have. They encouraged his passions in science and math, urged him to develop qualities of self-reliance, and nourished his sense of wonder.

LEARNING IS MESSY

Einstein was a strange boy who had trouble making friends and whose teachers considered him insubordinate and incompetent, and had he been of the fixed mindset he may well have believed them. But Einstein's growth mindset propelled him beyond failure, setbacks, and obstacles to new heights never before conceived of in science. Einstein defined insanity as "doing the same thing over and over again and expecting different results." When people of a fixed mindset make mistakes, they're often unwilling to change the behavior or action from which the mistake resulted or acknowledge a mistake was made at all. They avoid challenge and stay rooted in their comfort zone: never risking looking stupid, but forever missing out on new and different results. Growth mindset, on the other hand, is characterized by a willingness to try new strategies to find a better result.

The learning process is filled with mistakes and setbacks; it can be stifled by preconceived notions and interrupted by environmental challenges. Real learning in your classroom with twenty different kids and twenty different brains and twenty different perspectives is messy, loud, and unpredictable. Perhaps the only constant is that your students will make mistakes, but you can plan how you'll help students navigate those inevitable mistakes. Here's a three-step strategy for harnessing the power of mistakes in the classroom:

1. Normalize mistakes.

2. Value mistakes as learning opportunities.

3. Coach students through setbacks.

Normalize mistakes. At the beginning of the year, inform students they'll make mistakes and the mistakes will help them learn. Together create a "mistake language." In one classroom, the teacher and students say "Great mistake!" when they encounter a mistake that shows learning. In another, the teacher asks for a "mistake rationale" to get students to engage in metacognition, or thinking about their thinking. Another teacher calls her students "mistake mechanics." When a breakdown happens, the mechanics have to open the hood (the mind), pinpoint what went wrong, and come up with a strategy to fix it. Having a consistent process for tackling mistakes makes them feel routine and expected, not embarrassing and uncommon. Mistakes are so common in fact, you've planned for them!

There are millions of stories floating around the world of mistakes turned great inventions and failures turned wild successes. Using some of these stories in the form of bell work, journal prompts, or motivators is a great way to plant the seeds of failure being a natural part of hard work. J. K. Rowling, celebrated author of the *Harry Potter* books, was terrified of failure, before it happened to her. She found herself hitting a series of setbacks, including financial hardship, relationship trouble, and professional rejection, before she hit it big with her popular tales of young witches and wizards in training, and discovered that the failure, oddly enough, propelled her in ways that finding success never could have.

"So why do I talk about the benefits of failure? Simply because failure meant a stripping away of the inessential. I stopped pretending to myself that I was anything other than what I was and began to direct all my energy into finishing the only work that mattered to me," said Rowling, who went on to explain that, in hindsight, her personal and professional failures were ultimately a gift, because once she experienced and survived failure she was finally free of fearing it.[73]

Students need opportunities to experience failure at school so they understand that failing is not something to be covered up or feared, rather it is an important and natural experience from which they can learn.

Value mistakes as learning opportunities. Turning mistakes into valuable learning opportunities is also key to normalizing them. A popular video on TeachingChannel.org, a repository of instructional teaching videos, is "My Favorite No," in which a middle school math teacher, Leah Alcala, discusses a strategy she uses to demonstrate the value of mistakes.

At the beginning of her classes, Alcala posts a problem on the board and then hands out note cards on which the students will solve the problem. She collects the answers and quickly sorts them into a yes pile (the students who got it right) and a no pile (the students who got it wrong).

"I look for my favorite wrong answer or my favorite no, and then we analyze it," said Alcala.[74]

Alcala's "favorite no" is a wrong answer that demonstrates some solid math. She projects the wrong answer and asks the students to identify good thinking in the problem. At the end of the discussion, she asks the students to find the mistake. In Alcala's class, mistakes are not penalized; they're used as a jumping-off point for a discussion for improvement. Not all mistakes are created equal, however. Some mistakes, like errors born of rushed work, have no real value except to demonstrate that rushing through work results in errors. Alcala seizes on the mistakes that have learning value.

Coach students through setbacks. When students hit a snag in their learning they cannot resolve, the teacher has the opportunity to step in and coach them through it. Develop some coaching go-to strategies for students to deploy when they're struggling in learning. It's important that you don't fix the problem for the student; to benefit from the mistake, a student has to work through it. Here are some strategies that work for us:

STRATEGY	DESCRIPTION
ASK THREE THEN ASK ME	In this strategy, when students hit a snag, they must first ask three classmates to help them through it. This promotes collaboration in problem solving, and allows students the opportunity to use metacognitive strategies to think through a mistake or error.
OPEN-ENDED QUESTIONS	Develop a repertoire of open-ended questions you use to provoke problem-solving in struggling students. Questions like "Why do you think this happened?" or "What's another strategy you could use?" or "How might you avoid this mistake next time?" encourage students to think through the cause of the mistake and develop strategies to fix it. Tip: be comfortable with silence! Once you ask an open-ended question, give students time to answer. Too often, we try to jump in and answer the question when the silence has gone on too long. Wait them out!

REFLECTION JOURNAL	Give students time to reflect on their learning. The act of articulating what went well and what didn't through journaling will give students time to stop and process their learning. They may come up with insights in this process they may not have otherwise.
PREFLECTION ACTIVITIES	Before learning occurs ask students to think about potential obstacles. If they consider what areas of the concept, skill, or task might pose a problem beforehand, they'll be better prepared to handle any setbacks. This is also a way to normalize mistakes because it lets students know that you expect them to make mistakes in their learning.
USE THE MISTAKE AS PART OF THE LEARNING	If you see a great mistake—the kind that shows good process, but fails to meet its goal—make an example out of it! Like the strategy "My Favorite No," use mistakes as examples of how good process can go awry. Show the students the mistake and ask for input on what went wrong and how it can be repaired. This serves to both normalize mistakes and demonstrate important metacognitive strategies in thinking through problems.

FAMOUS MISTAKES
LESSON PLAN

LEARNING OBJECTIVES

By the end of the lesson, students will:

- conduct research and report on a famous mistake.
- demonstrate understanding of the value of mistakes.

RESOURCES AND MATERIALS

- Computers
- Internet
- Paper
- Writing utensils
- Poster paper
- Markers

METHOD

Say: "What do a microwave, potato chips, and Play-Doh have in common?" (Allow time for students to come up with responses.) Say: "Those are all interesting guesses, but the answer is that the microwave, potato chips, and Play-Doh were accidental inventions. Yes, you heard that right! All three products were created by mistake. In the case of Play-Doh, the doughy material made by Kutol Products was originally used to wipe soot off walls in the days when homes ran on coal stoves. Eventually people stopped using coal as a home heating source, and the company was going out of business until the owner found out that his sister, who was a teacher, was using it as a sort of modeling clay in her classroom. By the next year, Kutol Products turned into Rainbow Crafts, and has been marketing Play-Doh as a children's toy ever since. Sometimes in the course of our schoolwork we get a wrong answer or stumble upon a different strategy, or way of doing something, and these moments can be great learning opportunities! We already know mistakes help our brains grow, but they can also help us see things in a whole new way. Today, you'll use the Internet to research some familiar items that came about unintentionally or by mistake. You'll be assigned a topic (or choose one of your own!), research it, and fill out the mistake survey. After that, you'll create a poster about your invention to show others the value of mistakes."

Assign or have students/groups choose an item from the list to research. Use your classroom protocols for Internet research or guide students through the Google process. Googling "________ invented by mistake" or "________ invented by accident" will likely be enough to generate a good search result. Don't forget to have students evaluate the credibility of their source material!

THE GREAT MISTAKE LIST

Potato Chips	Super Glue	Popsicles
Microwave	Post-Its	Chocolate Chip Cookies
X-ray Images	Silly Putty	Velcro
Plastic	Penicillin	Ice Cream Cones
Teflon	Liquid Paper	Frisbee
Saccharin	Slinky	

Have students answer these questions during/after the research process:

1. How was the product created by mistake?
2. How do we use this product today?
3. How did learning about this mistake make you think differently about mistakes and challenges you face?

Now, have students create posters (or other presentations) depicting how the product was created by mistake and the value the mistake generated for society.

CHECK FOR UNDERSTANDING

Evaluate presentations to ensure that students have properly depicted the mistake and the value of the mistake.

NEXT-LEVEL MISTAKES: GAME NOT OVER

The cultural obsession with video games shows us that kids have the capacity to continually try for a goal even in the face of repeated failures, and yet many of the same children willing to spend hours mastering a level in a video game give up at the first sign of failure in school.

The mindset-researcher Lisa Blackwell writes, "In a video game, students are motivated by earning points, but they don't get discouraged when they fail. [The] video games involve skill, challenge, and incremental progress — without the threat of permanent failure or negative judgment from others."[75] This "threat of permanent failure" is taken away in video games, where the player is given an unlimited number of chances to improve. Every failed attempt at a level is still an incremental step toward the mastery of it. Teachers can take some clues from the gaming industry — masters at engaging kids — to provoke the same kind of stick-to-it-ness in the classroom that kids employ in video games. Try out some of these gaming-inspired strategies:

1. **Provide examples**. If you're curious how to conquer any level on any video game, all you need to do is check YouTube. Someone (or multiple people) have undoubtedly uploaded a video walking the player through how to beat a difficult level. Similarly, when teachers ask students to produce a piece of work, they should be able to offer examples of what an end product might look like. Rubrics, examples of past student work, and tutorials are ways to clearly indicate work product expectations.

2. **Nonthreatening**. In gaming, players often wear the amount of effort devoted to mastering a level or game like a badge of honor — "I played that level for five hours straight!" Similarly, students should be celebrated for how hard they work to master a concept or skill. Parents and teachers often celebrate a student's ability to master something quickly, though it can provoke negative consequences like fixed mindsets, cheating, and superficial learning. There's little consequence for failing a level in a video game: if you die, you just start again. Similarly, students should have room to fail without consequence. If they mess up, allow them to start again

where they are. All the learning shouldn't be chucked out just because at some point the student derailed.

3. **Student input.** In video games there's some element of choice. Players choose the style of game they want to play and can tackle challenges in various ways. Students should also have voice and choice when it comes to their schoolwork. Allow students input on the work they'll be doing and how it'll be assessed. This voice and choice will promote ownership over the task and help students self-motivate to succeed.

4. **Embrace differences.** Just as there are different strategies for mastering a video game, teachers should give students space to strategize ways to master a challenge. Not all students learn the same way, so a strategy that works for one student may not work for another. This is where the "not yet" comes in. Let students try multiple paths and figure out on their own what works and what doesn't. The process of discovery will be a far more meaningful experience than trying once and giving up.

5. **Intrinsic motivation.** Kids are completely self-motivated to play video games. There's no reward at the end; they're in it purely for fun and challenge. Likewise, students must be self-motivated in their schoolwork. Teachers who try to motivate students with external rewards are never as successful as teachers who help students discover what motivates them intrinsically.

6. **Cheats.** We know, we know, cheating is a dirty word in education, but there are all sorts of cheats and codes students can use in video games to give themselves a boost. We're not suggesting that you encourage students to cheat, but giving them tips and tricks to use as strategies in learning should be fair game! Dena, a high school English teacher, openly encourages her students to use SparkNotes, a kind of digital CliffsNotes when they don't get through a reading or need help understanding it. "I don't mind if kids use SparkNotes or access summaries of the readings I've assigned. It's just another way to get the story. If a student is struggling to understand *Macbeth*, I'd rather they Google a summary of it than abandon it all together. I want them to have multiple tools at their disposal, and I'm

not going to discount a student who needed a little help figuring out a storyline. I think it's resourceful."

7. **Constant feedback.** In a video game, the player is constantly receiving feedback. Dings, bells, and organ tones are consistently informing the player of everything good and bad happening along the way. In the same way, kids need a stream of feedback from teachers and peers offering valuable advice and information that can enhance their learning. A video game that required the player to blindly work his or her way through the level, and then doled out some too-little-too-late feedback at the end, would be an unpopular one. Same goes for student work. Feedback delivered throughout the process is more valuable than some notes on a test handed back a week later, long after the student has moved on.

8. **Scaffolding.** Video games build on one challenge after the other, increasing in difficulty. This sequencing creates a clear path to mastery: First, you have to get the sword. Then you have to get through the forbidden forest. Then you rescue the enchanted fairy. Many times teachers present concepts in isolation without giving students a roadmap of where they're going or why. Make sure that you provide support to students in the form of scaffolding information and skill acquisition, but not too much: nobody likes to play a game that isn't challenging.

9. **Create healthy competition.** Not all students are intrinsically motivated by competition, but many are. Using gamification strategies, teachers can use video games or other types of games to create camaraderie, increase engagement, and promote learning through game playing. This is often a popular strategy with students. Be cautious to promote cooperation as an essential component of competition; avoid giving prizes or making too big of a deal about scores. Have students work in groups to practice collaboration and avoid pitting student against student.

Clearly, the gaming industry knows a thing or two about engaging kids. Try some of these strategies to help promote can-do attitudes and resilience in tackling schoolwork that kids often demonstrate in gaming.

PRODUCTIVE FAILURE

When parents and teachers swoop in to protect children from failure, they do them a disservice by depriving them of the opportunity to learn how to fail in a way that's productive and meaningful. Knowing how to fail is valuable skill, and one that more and more children aren't mastering thanks to overprotective parents and self-esteem culture.

Some call it "failing up." Some call it "failing forward." Whatever you call it, productive failure is the idea that mistakes and setbacks can be transitioned into valuable learning opportunities. Manu Kapur, a professor of psychological studies at the Hong Kong Institute of Education, has dedicated his career to the study of productive failure. His research indicates that when students are given time to struggle with solving a problem, as opposed to receiving explicit instruction on how to solve it, they'll be able to better access and apply the information they learn in the struggle later on.[76]

Kapur conducted a study on the theory of productive failure in Singapore schools. In the study, two groups of students were exposed to two different strategies of mathematical instruction. The first group was given explicit instruction and clear feedback to solve a set of problems. A second group did not receive explicit instruction from a teacher but instead were directed to collaborate with peers to solve the problems, in lieu of asking the teacher for help. The students in the first group, with help from the teacher, were able to correctly answer the problems they had been given. The students in the second group, absent any instructional support from the teacher, were unable to get the problems right. However, Kapur recorded that the second group spent far more time discussing ideas, strategies, and various outcomes of the problem, and when he tested the groups on their learning, the second group did better than the first.

"Hidden efficacy" is how Kapur identifies this idea that struggle can propel students to deeper thinking about the nature of problems, which can be far more valuable than figuring correct sums.[77] If students have struggled their way through a problem to a solution, Kapur posits, they can better apply the hard-won solution the next time it's needed. This productive struggle, while uncomfortable in the moment, helps students develop better understandings about learning and problem solving. Teachers can incorporate six features in a lesson that will help create an environment ripe for productive struggle.[78]

1. The problems are challenging, but not to the point of frustration.
2. Tasks must have multiple solutions so students can generate many ideas. There cannot be only one way to get the right answer.
3. Productive failure design must activate students' prior knowledge, but students should not be able to solve the problem using only prior knowledge. It should include new challenges.
4. Students have opportunities to explain and elaborate on their thinking and strategies.
5. Students have a chance to examine both good and bad solutions to the problems.
6. The task should be relevant and engaging to students.

"The aim of teaching and learning is to go beyond the basics and engender deeper conceptual understanding and ability to transfer knowledge flexibly to new situations," writes Kapur.[79] This is why allowing for — and even planning for — failure in your lessons can provide such a powerful learning opportunity for your students; in negotiating the challenges you've created, they'll develop strategic and critical thinking skills useful in life.

Math, in particular, lends itself to incorporating the productive failure learning situations Kapur describes. Consider your own classroom or subject matter, and, keeping in mind the six characteristics of a productive failure task, come up with an idea for your own:

____

____

____

____

____

____

____

9

APRIL: THERE'S A DIFFERENCE BETWEEN NOT KNOWING AND NOT KNOWING YET!

Test scores and measures of achievement tell you where a student is, but they don't tell you where a student could end up.

—Carol Dweck

OBJECTIVES

- ✓ Formulate a plan to use the principle "not yet" in your classroom.
- ✓ Distinguish between formative and summative assessments.
- ✓ Learn strategies and activities that emphasize value in the learning process.

NOT YET

In Carol Dweck's heavily viewed TED Talk, "The Power of Believing That You Can Improve," she tells a story about a high school in Chicago where students received the grade "not yet" if they didn't pass a class.

"I thought that was fantastic," said Dweck, "because if you get a failing grade, you think, I'm nothing, I'm nowhere. But if you get the grade 'not yet,' you understand that you're on a learning curve. It gives you a path into the future."[80]

A lot can be read into that word: FAIL. There's something so definite about it; unlike "mistake" or "setback," the finality of the word implies your goose is cooked. Over. Finito. Dunzo. But the word *yet*? Now, that's a magical word. *Yet* conveys the promise of better things to come. *Yet* is the future saying, "Hey, you! I'm right up here. Come and get me!" Replacing failing grades with "not yet" proved to be a revolutionary strategy for that school in Chicago, and other schools and teachers are following suit.

A high school math teacher in Oklahoma, Sarah Carter, who was profiled as one of NPR's 50 Great Teachers in 2015,[81] is an example of a teacher who has embraced the growth mindset. Her classroom features a bulletin board, which turns common fixed-mindset phrases into growth-oriented ones. "This is too hard" becomes "This may take some time and effort." "I made a mistake" becomes "Mistakes help me learn." And "It's good enough" becomes "Is this really my best work?" Instead of grading her students with the traditional A through F scale, Carter hands out As, Bs, or "not yet."

"You either get an A, a B, or a not yet," one of Carter's students told NPR. Other students relayed stories of Carter giving them opportunities to take quizzes again and do assignments over until they arrived in A or B territory.

On her blog, Math = Love, Carter posted some student responses to her grading system. One student said that the class was hard, but the grading system was ultimately helpful. Another wrote, "The grading scale may seem like it sucks, but she will help you by letting you redo your work. It actually helps you learn the material better."[82]

There you have it, from the mouth of a teenager. The concept of not yet — much like embracing mistakes and relishing failure — may kind of "suck" at first, but, ultimately, it propels students to greater understanding.

Ask Yourself: How can you incorporate the principle of not yet in your classroom?

GROWTH-MINDED ASSESSMENT

Assessment can do a number on a student's growth mindset. That's why it's important that assessment practices reflect the values of instructional practice. In other words, if you take a growth-mindset approach to teaching, you shouldn't be using assessment methods in a way that feeds the fixed mindset. The two most popular types of assessments are:

FORMATIVE ASSESSMENT: An assessment administered periodically throughout a unit of study as part of the instructional process. Results are often used to make instructional decisions, determine if reteaching or extensions to the lesson need to be addressed, guide learning experiences in the class, and provide opportunity for student reflection. Formative assessment offers timely feedback during learning when necessary adjustments can be made.

SUMMATIVE ASSESSMENT: An assessment used to evaluate a student's learning at the end of a unit of study. Summative assessments often come in the form of tests, ranging from chapter tests to high-stakes tests, like state assessments. Summative assessment offers data on student achievement in relationship to benchmarks and standards.

Here are some examples of formative and summative assessments.

FORMATIVE ASSESSMENT	SUMMATIVE ASSESSMENT
Homework/Practice	Piano recital
Bell work/Exit slips	Final exam
Self assessment/Peer assessment	State assessment
Journal writing	Research paper final
Metacognitive activities	End-of-unit exam

Formative assessment is embedded in learning. Formative assessment gauges the day-to-day progress that shows students where they are in relationship to where they need to be. Formative assessment allows us to help our students chart a clear path to mastery. Summative assessment, in the traditional sense, is none of these things. Summative assessment enters at the end of learning and gives an analytical measure of progress based on a student's performance on the assessment.

Summative assessments don't have the nuance and narrative that formative assessments do. Summative assessment tells us how a particular student fared taking a test on a particular day, but doesn't give us a holistic view of how the student has progressed through the learning. Sometimes it's an accurate reflection of student learning, but sometimes it's not. And yet, most teachers, administrators, parents, and students put a lot of stock into those summative assessments. After all, that's where the grades come from, right?

Teachers can and should incorporate growth mindset in both formative and summative assessments. If you change the way you praise students to focus on the process, but continue assessing students in the same manner that emphasizes the value of performance over the value of process, your students won't truly reap the benefits of a growth-oriented classroom. If you want to embrace growth mindset in your classroom, you have to put your money, or in this case your *grades*, where your mouth is. Let's take a look at what growth-oriented formative and summative assessment looks like in a middle school math classroom.

Shelley Sopha, a middle school math teacher in Kansas City, Kansas, says assessments are most valuable when they are valid, reliable, and give immediate feedback. She points out that students can develop a growth mindset toward classroom assessment, particularly if they're given the opportunity to retake the assessment to demonstrate learning.

"If the classroom teacher designs an environment that honors and celebrates a growth mindset, kids will want to keep taking assessments and won't settle with not doing well," says Sopha.[83]

She points out that when summative assessment is closely aligned with formative assessment, there should be no mystery on how a student will do on a summative assessment. Formative assessment also doesn't have to be — and shouldn't be — retaking the same test over and over again, but students who need more opportunities to demonstrate progress can show that in other ways like correcting the test, teaching the material to another student or the teacher, writing a new version of the test and answering it, or completing other student-generated forms of assessment.

Sopha thinks that it's possible to use high-stakes summative assessment to foster growth mindset, but only if kids are tracking their scores year to year. She does a version of this in her class in which students take a yearly pretest and posttest, so they can see a concrete example of their growth.

"In my experience, kids are willing to give their very best effort on high-stakes tests if they feel like they can't fail and they understand that progress is the goal," says Sopha. "MAP testing, for example, is taken two or three times a year, and measures growth. Kids feel a sense of accomplishment when the test shows they've grown. The test isn't perfect, but it at least shows that we value and celebrate growth."[84]

For Sopha, designing and organizing tests in a way that supports growth mindset is key. She doesn't worry about scores, percentages, or grades, but focuses on tracking progress toward mastery on specific standards. Instead of assigning an A through F grade on the standards, she tracks learning by indicating where the work falls on this spectrum: remediation needed, basic understanding, near mastery, mastery. Then she gives students as many opportunities as necessary to practice and demonstrate learning.

"If kids are putting in the time and effort, it should never count against them," says Sopha. "They should never be penalized for practice, which may see obvious, but you'd be surprised at how many teachers grade homework and classwork, and then have those scores reflected in the student's grade. Grading is fine, but the students should always have a chance to increase their score."[85]

This type of mastery grading — indicating where the student falls on a spectrum of progress toward mastery — allows students to monitor their progress and provides more opportunities for students to be involved in making choices about both the type and modality of their learning. When learners know that they can retake exams, it can change motivation. If they receive feedback that shows they haven't yet demonstrated mastery, it doesn't mean that they've capital-F Failed, it just means that they have more work to do. And no one is in a better position than the student to determine what will help most in progressing toward mastery.

Sopha, who is transitioning to a school counseling position next year, says instilling a growth mindset in the classroom aligns closely with the core conditions needed in counseling for growth and change.

"In my mind," says Sopha, "with a warm caring climate, meaningful relationships and connections to others, students want to grow and develop a way of being that seeks exploration and a better understanding of self, others, and the world. The environment fosters a growth mindset, and everything we do as teachers can either cultivate or hinder that development."[86]

A CRISIS OF SIGNIFICANCE

Kelly, a high school teacher, tells a story from her teaching experience:

> *"Every time I gave my high school students an assignment, hands would shoot up across the classroom all wanting to know one thing: "How many points is this worth?" I would get so frustrated, I would say: "Ten billion!" or some other ridiculous point value. I desperately wanted them to understand it wasn't the amount of arbitrary points they could get out of their work that was important; it was what they were learning. But they had been conditioned in all of their other classes to worry about the points, and it was really hard to get them to think about their schoolwork in a different way."*

Kelly's problem is not a unique one. Many schools place a premium on how many points kids can earn: the "valedictorian" award goes to the student with the highest grade point average, scholarships are awarded to the students with the most points on their SAT, and so on. Even if your school culture is one that values summative results, you can still create a growth-oriented environment in your classroom by engaging in activities and strategies that show your students that you value the learning process more than a grade on a final exam.

Have you ever noticed that when you pass back a quiz or exam to a classroom full of students, they immediately start comparing their grades to one another? Those with the As proudly wave their tests around, while those with the Ds and Fs shrink in their chairs, hoping not to become the target of other students looking to find someone who did worse than them.

On the flip side, if you tell students—especially middle and high school students—that something will not be graded, many of them lose the will to engage in it. If it's not for points, the logic goes, then what's the point? In our culture, saying someone is an "A student" might as well be synonymous with "good person." So it's really no wonder that we have reaped what we've sown: a school system so entrenched in the grading culture that our stressed-out students, studies have shown, would rather compromise their integrity by cheating than lose a few lousy points.

Michael Wesch, a professor of anthropology at Kansas State University, contends that educators must seek to provide learning experiences in which students are not passive receivers of knowledge but active seekers of answers to questions that mean something to them. He calls this problem of students working to pass tests and get points at school a crisis of significance.

"Consider the often-heard lament, 'some students are just not cut out for school.' The statement passes without question or even a hint of protest, yet think about what the statement says when we replace 'school' with what school should be all about: 'learning.' Some students are just not cut out for learning? Nobody would dare make that statement," Wesch writes in an article for *Education Canada*.[87] He goes on to say that if students are feeling disenfranchised or uncomfortable in the school system we've created, it may because we've drawn the boundaries too narrowly. A more inclusive learning environment that appeals to and includes a more diverse range of people and ideas is beneficial to everyone.

In many ways, Wesch says, modern schools haven't kept up with the digital revolution. Prior to fifteen years ago, the amount of knowledge students had access to was limited to what their teacher knew or what was available in the library. Now, students have access to the entirety of human knowledge at their fingertips, so the *what* of learning is far less important than the *why* or *how*. It's mind-boggling to think that the developments in both the amount of information available to us and the efficacy with which we can access it hasn't really changed our approach to education all that much.

"As we increasingly move toward an environment of instant and infinite information, it becomes less important for students to know, memorize, or recall information, and more important for them to be able to find, sort, analyze, share, discuss, critique, and create information," writes Wesch.[88] He says that we need to stop focusing on whether students are knowledgeable and help them become "knowledge-able."

Moving students from knowledgeable to knowledge-able means presenting them with authentic learning opportunities from which they can both find answers and generate more questions. We should be inspiring in our students curiosity about the world, not about how many points they need to get an A. Here are some ideas for creating knowledge-able tasks in your classroom.

KNOWLEDGEABLE (WHAT)	KNOWLEDGE-ABLE (WHY/HOW)
Memorize the state capitals.	Produce a documentary about a state capital.
Find the vocabulary words in a word search.	Write a fiction piece using all the vocabulary words.
Name the dinosaurs in the Jurassic Period.	Project-based learning: What would a world in which humans and dinosaurs coexist look like?
Label the diagram of the insect life cycle.	Film a video depicting a day in the life of an insect (bumblebee, ant, etc.).
Learn about energy efficiency.	Design a test for insulation materials to determine the best one.
Figure the area of the playground.	Design a playground.
List three reasons why an animal is endangered.	Design a plan to preserve an endangered species.
Tell how a bill becomes a law.	Design a mock legislative session to demonstrate how a bill becomes a law.
Write a report on Gettysburg.	Create a podcast from the front lines of Gettysburg.

Project-based learning is a way to incorporate knowledge-able work with high value to the students. According to the Buck Institute for Education (BIE), project-based learning is "a teaching method in which students gain knowledge and skills by working for an extended period of time to investigate and respond to an engaging and complex question, problem, or challenge."[89]

Whether you've heard it called inquiry-based learning, challenge-based learning, or problem-based learning, the goal is essentially the same: provide students with authentic, real-world problems on which they must use deep thinking and collaborative skills to solve. These kinds of tasks take learning out of the abstract to give students a real opportunity to come up with solutions to issues that affect them.

BIE, known for its work in project-based learning in education, has outlined eight features of "gold-standard" project design.

Here are eight features of "gold-standard" PBL.[90]

FEATURE	DESCRIPTION
KEY KNOWLEDGE, UNDERSTANDING, AND SUCCESS SKILLS	Content and standards-based knowledge are embedded in the overall design of the project, and the project cultivates important skills like problem solving, critical thinking, self-management, and collaborative group work.
CHALLENGING PROBLEM OR QUESTION	An open-ended question provides the framework for the project. It must be meaningful to the students, be challenging to answer (students shouldn't be able to Google the answer!), and be sufficiently challenging.
SUSTAINED INQUIRY	This is not a one-day task! A project should include research, resource gathering, application, and creation. It'll take at least three weeks.
AUTHENTICITY	The project should have real-world application and be relevant to student interests and issues that affect them.
STUDENT VOICE AND CHOICE	Students have the opportunity to guide most aspects of their project like team strategy and final design.
REFLECTION	Reflection is embedded in the process. Students and teachers engage in metacognitive reflection about obstacles, phases of the project, teamwork, quality of the work, etc.
CRITIQUE AND REVISION	Students value both teacher and peer feedback as part of making improvements to their process or product.
PUBLIC PRODUCT	Students make their work public by way of presentation or otherwise making it available to an audience beyond the classroom.

Project-based learning and other types of learning activities that ask students to solve problems relevant to their lives are important for several reasons. First, real-world questions and solutions are relevant to students' lives, which increases their engagement with the learning at hand. Second, much of the work they'll do as adults will be completing projects, so it's important that they practice the various skills necessary to that kind of work. Finally, it gives students a chance to direct their own learning, problem-solve obstacles and setbacks, and practice essential skills like feedback and reflection—all features of authentic work that cultivate and strengthen growth mindsets.

FORMATIVE ASSESSMENT STRATEGIES

There are many more ways to gather formative assessment information than by administering a quiz. Here are a few ways to incorporate formative assessment strategies into your growth-oriented classroom. These strategies will help guide the process of learning in your classroom by engaging your students in tasks to help them examine their learning and by providing you an opportunity to reflect on your instruction. Whenever possible, engage students in collaborative formative assessment. Following are some formative assessment strategies:

STRATEGY	DESCRIPTION
REFLECTION RX	After a formative assessment ask students to write an RX, a reflection prescription, about what steps they'll take to improve in areas of struggle.
PEER ASSESSMENT AND FEEDBACK	Students give process critiques to their peers to help them advance their learning.
DIGITAL CHECK-INS	Use real-time creation tools like Google Docs and Google Slides to check in on your students' progress, ask questions, and offer feedback as they are working on projects and tasks.
NEARPOD LESSONS	Incorporate lessons, videos, surveys, and Q&A slides to gather input.
PEER SHARING	Listen as students explain their learning, understanding, and misconceptions to their shoulder partners.

STRATEGY	DESCRIPTION
SMALL GROUP SESSIONS	Use guided group instruction to evaluate student understanding and to reteach, clarify, or extend lessons. Students should use this time to ask and answer questions about their learning and reflect on their understanding. These pieces help guide instruction.
SORTS (WORDS, DEFINITIONS, ANALOGIES, PICTURES)	Sorts can be used to determine whether students understand the concepts and to identify where more learning is needed.
CENTERS	Allow students to explore their learning through center tasks. These tasks will help students identify areas of confusion or the need for extension.
DIGITAL RESPONSE SERVICES OR SYSTEMS	Clickers, Socrative Teacher, Polls Everywhere, and survey questions can be used to gather students' insights and understanding to guide instruction.
EXIT FORMS	Before leaving the classroom, students jot down the answer to one or more of the following prompts: I learned . . . Questions I still have include . . . I can apply my learning to . . . I connected to . . . Things I found interesting include . . . I want to know . . .
SELF-REFLECTION	Students evaluate their understanding using a learning scale to determine where they need more instruction or to identify obstacles.
GRAPHIC ORGANIZERS	Advance organizers help students organize information and can be used to assess student schema prior to learning.
SLATE WORK	Use individual white boards for Q&A sessions or for students to work through problems or clarify student learning. Students share their thinking while the teacher facilitates around the room.
DIAGRAMS	Students model their understanding by creating diagrams and models.
HIGHLIGHTING	Highlighting confusing areas or mistakes in student work encourages students to make clarifications and corrections.

A BETTER WAY TO GRADE

We said before that assigning grades during formative assessment unfairly penalizes students when they're still in the process of learning. Many teachers argue that grades on formative assessments help them track where students are in their learning, but there are many alternatives to achieve that.

Letting students know where they fall on a spectrum in regard to how well they're learning a skill or concept in class is a good way to assess learning without having to attach a grade to it, like Carter's strategy of A, B, or not yet, or Sopha's spectrum of remediation needed, basic understanding, near mastery, mastery. Teachers can also assign levels of understanding a number, color, letter, or some other designation, and have students evaluate their own learning. For example, a student learning scale might look something like this:

Green — I've got it and I can teach it!

Yellow — I get some of this, but I need more practice.

Red — Stop! I don't understand this yet.

In this scenario, the students would indicate whether they considered themselves a green, yellow, or red in terms of the learning goal. The teacher could then use that information to inform small group instruction or other means of learning.

Teachers should not be the only source of feedback on formative assessments. Students should be using metacognitive tools to self-assess their own learning. Asking students to engage in reflective assessment is an excellent way to improve their metacognition — or thinking about their thinking — and help them develop skills of self-assessment that will serve them in future learning situations. Here's an example of a "think sheet" that uses stems to guide students in metacognitive self-assessment.

THINK SHEET

I'm still wondering ______________________________

I understand ______________________________

My learning is connected to ______________________________

I can apply my learning ______________________________

A confusing part was ______________________________

I think I'll understand it better if ______________________________

If I don't grasp a concept, I can ______________________________

In *Mindset,* Carol Dweck describes a study in which she and her colleagues surveyed teachers by asking them how they would treat a student who had received a 65 percent on a math test. Many teachers taking the survey were able to draw conclusions about the student as a person from the test grade, as well as offer many recommendations on how to handle the situation. One teacher wrote Dweck an angry letter, insisting that his survey not be included in her study. He was upset that the survey dared to ask teachers to make a judgment about a student based only on a single grade. Little did he know, many of his colleagues were more than happy to make those judgments. Dweck, of course, agreed with the angry letter writer.

"An assessment at one point in time has little value for understanding someone's ability, let alone their potential to succeed in the future," writes Dweck, who goes on to explain how the urgency associated with assessments can make students feel as if there's no time to learn the material or stumble over difficult concepts. A classroom culture that heavily values high-level assessment performance may be promoting the idea that students need to be as perfect as possible as quickly as possible if they want to be considered successful or smart.

There's such a thing as a growth-mindset approach to assessment, and it centers on valuing mistakes, struggle, and growth. The reality is that high-stakes assessments and letter grades probably aren't going away anytime soon, but there are steps teachers can take to prevent students from viewing grades as a direct reflection on their intelligence and instead see them as a measure of progress. Here are some strategies teachers can use to provide more authentic, holistic assessment.

STRATEGY	DESCRIPTION
ALTERNATE SCALE	Instead of the traditional A–F scale, try developing a scale that focuses on process and encourages mastery. Try this: Advancing Developing Not yet
RUBRICS	A rubric, especially ones that emphasizes process over product, provides students with a roadmap rather than a recipe.
NARRATIVE REPORTS	Teachers write a narrative report in lieu of or alongside a grade.
STUDENT-LED CONFERENCES	Student-led conferences allow students to share their goals, process of learning, obstacles, and progress with their parents. When the student is excluded from the conference, the conversation will often default to grades. Including the student in the conference focuses the conversation on his or her experiences, feelings, thoughts, and opinions. This can offer more insight than a grade on a report.

Andrew Kasprisin, a science teacher at Essex Middle School in Essex, Vermont, wrote online about his school's move to a standards-based grading system.[91] He recounted how the principal of his school asked the teachers to sort note cards with student names into piles based on grades. Kasprisin said that the teachers noticed that the students earning As and Bs in class were considered the "good" students in school, the ones who always turned in their homework and asked for help when they needed it. Not so with the students in the C, D, and F piles. Those students often failed to turn in work and were perceived as low-achieving.

After this sorting exercise, the principal asked the teachers to rearrange the note cards again, but this time into three piles. Each pile represented either meeting, exceeding, or below standard. Interestingly, some of the "good" students in the A or B piles were now finding their way into the "below standard" pile. And some students who had low grades were now in the "exceeds standard" pile.

After some conversation, the teachers realized that the traditional grading system wasn't painting a good picture of what the students really knew. Soon, the school made a shift to standards-based grading. There was a period of transition in the new system: Kasprisin says that they had to keep reminding students and parents that this change would put the focus back on learning. For the teachers, this meant really considering what meeting standards looks like and working together to develop a plan.

"My written comments to students now more effectively point them in the right direction," writes Kasprisin, "and more and more, [my comments] are questions prompting my students to go deeper with their thinking."[92]

Standards-based grading, and other styles of growth-oriented assessment, have the power to help put the focus back on learning. There are so many creative ways to evaluate student work that can foster curiosity, increase motivation, and encourage deep thinking. When grades become less about how quickly and how perfectly a student can complete an assignment, we move nearer to the idea that, regardless of where our starting point may be, we all have room to grow.

10

MAY: I GOT THIS!

The path to growth mindset is a journey, not a proclamation.

—Carol Dweck

OBJECTIVES

- ✓ Understand how self-talk plays a role in developing growth mindset.
- ✓ Develop a growth-mindset plan to learn something new.
- ✓ Develop a growth-mindset plan to solve a problem.

There's a well-known Cherokee legend that tells the story of a grandfather talking to his grandson about life.[93] The grandfather tells the grandson that he has two wolves inside him. One wolf is evil—it is greed, envy, hatred, arrogance, and darkness. The other wolf is good—it is generosity, hope, love, humility, and light. These two wolves—the good and the evil—are at battle within all people, the grandfather tells his grandson.

The grandson looks at the grandfather and asks, "Which wolf wins?"

And the grandfather replies, "The one you feed."

Like the two wolves in the old legend, the fixed and growth mindsets are alive in our heads jockeying for position. Just as your growth mindset is feeling satisfied with a hard day's work, your fixed mindset swoops in and undermines it by asking, "But was it good enough?"

WHY WE SHOULD PRACTICE TALKING TO OURSELVES

Our inner voices are constantly buzzing away in our brains, and psychologists have discovered that what the voices are saying can have an impact on our success or failure. Lev Vygotsky, an early twentieth-century psychologist, called the self-talk of very young children "private speech." Observe a toddler alone at play, and you'll likely hear an audible narration of the events taking place, which Vygotsky believed was the very young child's effort to make sense of the world. Eventually that private speech turns into an inner monologue, or self-talk, working hard to organize thoughts, regulate behavior, and develop self-awareness. It's important to talk about inner voices with kids. Sometimes kids don't even realize that everyone else has an inner voice too!

Wesley, a five-year-old boy, approached his teacher and confessed to hitting another student on the playground. He said that he felt bad for what he had done in anger and felt like he should come clean. "Ah," the teacher said, "that little voice in your head knew you did something wrong, huh?" He looked at her wide-eyed, incredulous, and said, "How do *you* know about the voice in my head?"

Self-talk is critical to managing mindsets. Perhaps the best way to help students manage their mindsets is to help them develop an awareness of the fixed-mindset voices and growth-mindset voices in their heads. Once they can figure out which mindset the voice is coming from, they can work to reframe it.

One way to develop awareness of the fixed and growth mindsets is to ask your students to think of a time they were really frustrated and gave up at something. First give an example from your own life.

When I was in high school, I was playing in the finals match of a tennis tournament. My opponent in the final match was ranked the number one player in the state. She was bigger than me and had a much better record. This is what my fixed mindset was saying in my head:

She's bigger than you and can hit much harder.

There is no way you're going to beat her.

You might as well quit now before you get humiliated.

It's going to feel really bad when you get beaten.

Then ask your students how you could have responded to that fixed mindset voice with a growth-mindset voice. Make a T-chart with your fixed-mindset voice on one side and ask the students to devise some "comebacks" in a growth-mindset voice.

MY FIXED MINDSET	FIX MY FIXED MINDSET!
She's bigger than me.	I have played people bigger than me before, and won!
She hits harder than me.	I'll have to be extra quick to return her serves.
There's no way I'm going to beat her.	I'll work hard to try and win the game.
I might as well quit now before I get beaten.	Playing my hardest with dignity is more important than winning.
I'm going to feel bad when I lose.	Whether I win or lose, taking on this challenge will make me a better player.
She's ranked number one.	Rankings aren't set in stone; if I work hard, I could be number one.
This is too hard.	No matter what, I'll learn from this experience.
I'll never be that good.	Playing tough competitors helps me grow my ability.
Everyone will think I'm a loser.	People who care about me will support me no matter what.

Once your students understand how to differentiate between growth and fixed voices, ask them to work together to create T-charts of how their fixed mindset might try to sabotage them this summer, and how they can respond with a growth mindset.

MY FIXED MINDSET	FIX MY FIXED MINDSET!
I'll never learn to swim.	I should ask my parents if I can take swimming lessons, so I can learn to swim.
I'll never be as good at softball as Jenny.	Jenny is great at softball. I should ask her to practice with me.
There's no way I'm going to finish that entire summer reading list.	I'm going to tackle this list one book at a time.
Summer school is a waste of my time.	Summer school is my chance to improve some things I've been struggling with.
I didn't make the summer basketball team because I stink.	I didn't make the team this year, but I'll work hard, practice, and try again next year.
I'm not going to work on math this summer because I'll never be good.	Choices I make this summer may help me in math class next school year.
I'm glad school is out. I hate it.	I have to attend school, so I should try to focus on what's good about it and how I can make it better.

The pop superstar Beyoncé once told reporters that to overcome her natural shyness, she developed a stage persona she named Sasha Fierce. Whenever she went on stage, she mentally transformed into her alter ego, in order to give her the confidence she needed to deliver a powerful performance.

It's sometimes hard for students to conceptualize ideas that they can't name, which is why giving our fixed mindsets a name is a great way to develop a certain level of control over them. Just as Beyoncé named her alter ego Sasha Fierce in order to summon it before a big performance, your students can name their fixed mindsets in order to better respond. Once students have a good understanding of the fixed and growth mindsets, ask them to give their fixed mindsets a name. It's especially fun if they can give it a silly name. Here are some examples:

Negative Nelly

Stinky Cheese Man

Debbie Downer

The students can have a little fun naming their fixed mindsets, and once they've adopted the perfect moniker, they can start addressing the fixed mindset directly. You'll start hearing things like, "Uh-oh, Negative Nelly is talking to me." Or, "Go away, Stinky Cheese Man, I don't want to listen to you."

It may seem a little silly, but even Carol Dweck agrees that naming the fixed mindset is an excellent vehicle for communicating with it.[94] Just like we want our kids to tell a bully to go away and leave them alone, allowing students to name their fixed mindset gives them a tool to use when they respond to fixed-mindset messages. Sometimes it's important to validate the fixed mindset's fears, and then ask it to put those fears aside and take a leap with your growth mindset.

Another great way to take control of your fixed and growth mindsets is to come up with a sort of catchphrase that you can use to help get back on the right path. It might be something motivational, like "I know I can do this!" Or it might be a point of clarification, like "This challenge is helping me grow."

Here's a list of strategies students can use to manage their fixed-mindset voices:

STRATEGY	DESCRIPTION
NAME YOUR FIXED MINDSET	Have students name their fixed mindset. When their fixed-mindset voice says, "You know, it would be much easier to quit right now," they could say, "Buzz off, Buddy!" right back at it.
ROLE-PLAYING THE MINDSETS	Help students prepare for dealing with fixed mindset in others by having them write vignettes or skits and act them out. For example, students might write a skit with a fixed-mindset adult saying, "It's okay, not everyone is good at algebra." And a student responding, "I'm not good at algebra, yet, but with lots of hard work, I will be."
ACCOUNTABILITY PARTNERS	Have students team up as accountability partners and pledge to help foster each other's growth mindset. If your partner is buckling under the pressure of fixed-mindset messages, give him or her a growth-mindset pep talk.
DRAW YOUR FIXED MINDSET	Putting words and pictures to your fixed mindset is a great way to conceptualize it. This exercise will help students better recognize when they are in the fixed mindset, and once you can recognize it, it's much easier to control it.
PICK A GROWTH MINDSET CATCHPHRASE	Studies have shown that coming up with a catchphrase can help athletes get their heads back in the game. In the same way, students who feel that they're slipping into their fixed mindset can use a go-to catchphrase as a psychological cue to get back in the growth mindset. (Our monthly mantra — I got this! — is a good one.)
LETTER TO MY FIXED MINDSET	Have students write a letter to their fixed mindsets from their growth mindsets.

GROWTH MINDSET PLAN

In the final chapter of *Mindset*, Dweck writes of the importance of developing a plan of attack for using the growth mindset.[95] Dweck says that making a plan and visualizing how you'll carry it out will help you use the growth mindset when faced with failure and struggle, bad situations that can easily knock you off course if you let them.

Help students write their own plans for how they'll use growth mindset. Walk through developing two growth-mindset plans for the summer. The first will focus on something new they would like to learn over the summer (swimming, cooking, playing chess, etc.). The second will help them address a problem they might be having (getting along with a sibling, improving their reading level, etc.).

MY GROWTH-MINDSET PLAN FOR LEARNING

I want to learn ______________________________

My deadline for this is ______________________________

The resources I need to do this are ______________________________

____

I will accomplish this by ______________________________

____

Barriers to my learning are ______________________________

____

I will overcome barriers by ______________________________

____

If I make a mistake, I will ______________________________

My fixed mindset might say ______________________________

My growth mindset will respond ______________________________

Here are some ways I'll know that I've shown growth:

1. ______________________________

____

2. ______________________________

____

3. ______________________________

____

MY GROWTH-MINDSET PLAN FOR LEARNING (SAMPLE)

I want to learn how to play the French horn.

My deadline for this is end of summer.

The resources I need to do this are A French horn and a teacher, YouTube tutorials, books.

I'll accomplish this by practicing one hour every day, attending summer band camp, and practicing with my friend who plays the French horn.

Barriers to my learning are I won't have enough free time to practice for an hour. My neighbors might get annoyed at the noise. I can't afford a tutor.

I'll overcome barriers by making a set schedule so I don't forget to practice. I'll practice while neighbors are working. I'll do extra chores to earn money.

If I make a mistake, I'll ask for help and remind myself I'm making progress.

My fixed mindset might say You'll never learn how to play the French horn, just give up!

My growth mindset will respond If I keep working hard, I'll keep getting better.

Here are some ways I'll know I've shown growth:

1. I've learned the basic notes.
2. I've learned to play two songs.
3. I can make a YouTube video explaining French horn basics.

MY GROWTH-MINDSET PLAN FOR FACING A PROBLEM

My problem is ______________________________

I'll resolve my problem by this date: ______________________________

The resources I need to solve my problem are ______________________________

____

____

I'll solve my problem by ______________________________

____

____

Barriers to solving my problem are ______________________________

____

____

I'll overcome barriers by______________________________

____

____

If my plan doesn't work, I'll ______________________________

My fixed mindset might say ______________________________

My growth mindset will respond ______________________________

Here are some ways I'll know I've solved my problem:

1. ______________________________

____

2. ______________________________

____

3. ______________________________

____

MY GROWTH-MINDSET PLAN FOR FACING A PROBLEM (SAMPLE)

My problem is I am two grade levels behind in reading.

I'll resolve my problem by this date: By the start of the next school year.

The resources I need to solve my problem are reading materials from my teacher; Help from friends, teachers, or parents. Online resources for reading practice.

I'll solve my problem by asking my teacher to help me make a plan to improve my reading skills and practicing every day.

Barriers to solving my problem are I might not feel like practicing. I met get stuck or frustrated.

I'll overcome barriers by reminding myself that practice is key to improving my reading or trying to read books that really interest me, like Harry Potter, so I'll want to read.

If my plan doesn't work, I'll ask my teacher for a new strategy to improve reading.

My fixed mindset might say You'll never be a good reader. Just give up!

My growth mindset will respond I can improve my reading. It'll just take effort, practice, and time.

Here are some ways I'll know I have solved my problem.

1. I'll be able to understand more of what I read.

2. I'll be able to read a hard book without asking for help.

3. I'll be able to get to a higher level on my reading game online.

DETERMINING YOUR TRIGGERS

Part of developing a plan for students to use growth mindset moving forward is helping them identify the specific actions, behaviors, and situations that trigger their fixed mindsets.

"If we watch carefully for our fixed-mindset triggers, we can begin the true journey to a growth mindset," writes Dweck in *Education Week*.[96]

Work with students to make a list of "triggers" so you can be prepared to meet them head-on with a growth mindset. The list might include the following situations: when I lose my temper, when I feel like giving up, when I'm not in the mood to be at school, when I feel like I'm under a lot of pressure, or when I feel anxiety about how I'm performing. By naming these situations together, students may be better prepared to face them when they happen.

MY FIXED-MINDSET TRIGGERS

1. ______________________________

____

2. ______________________________

____

3. ______________________________

____

4. ______________________________

____

5. ______________________________

____

The act of planning and preparing for potential setbacks is an excellent way to stay in the growth mindset. If students have outlined a plan of action for when they feel themselves sinking into the fixed mindset, they'll be ready to initiate the plan to combat those feelings of failure and hopelessness with their growth-mindset strategies. This doesn't mean that their fixed mindsets will go away — the fixed mindset is always there with us — it just means that students will be better equipped to use growth-mindset strategies to overcome a problem or take on a new learning challenge.

SAYING GOOD-BYE

The end of the school year is bittersweet. It's been a long, hard year. You've laughed, you've cried, and you've come to know and love these interesting, complex individuals who've called your classroom home these past ten months. It's hard to let them go, but feel confident in knowing that by imparting to your students the power of growth mindset and the knowledge of how their brains have the capacity to grow and change with effort, you've given them a valuable tool they can access going forward. This knowledge will help students view effort and challenge through a lens of improvement and personal growth and not failure and personal shortcomings.

After *Mindset* became wildly popular, Dweck realized that some people were missing the point. Teachers were "banning" fixed mindset in the classroom, but that's counterintuitive. Everyone has a fixed mindset and a growth mindset, and this year you've helped students foster their growth mindsets in tremendous ways. But, you must remember, their fixed mindsets will always be there. There's no making a fixed mindset go away. What we can do is give students the tools to use their growth mindset to help them improve. If we turn having the "best" growth mindset into another competition or way to perform, we're really only stoking fixed mindsets: *What if my teacher doesn't think I have a good enough growth mindset?! Maria's growth mindset is better than mine, I'm such a loser compared to her. My teacher will think I'm stupid if I have a fixed mindset!*

There are so many factors that affect students' mindsets day to day. We cannot rid them of a fixed mindset, we can only hope to give them a set of strategies to help them avoid getting bogged down in failure, becoming scared of taking on challenges, and thinking they're somehow incapable or not biologically or intellectually meant to do, learn, or accomplish something. This shift in belief structure, however, can occur only when conditions support it. How can children adopt new beliefs about their power to improve if we continue to feed them a steady diet of person praise, performance tasks, and persecution of mistakes and failures?

Send your students to the next grade level or out in the world knowing that you gave them a tool that can help them overcome obstacles and challenges their whole lives long. And, in the process, you've likely developed your growth mindset, too.

11

JUNE: I CAN'T TAKE CARE OF OTHERS IF I DON'T TAKE CARE OF MYSELF

Your vision will become clear
only when you can look into your own heart.
Who looks outside, dreams; who looks inside, awakes.
—Carl Jung

OBJECTIVES

- ✓ Engage in a guided journaling reflection on your year of growth mindset.
- ✓ Create a plan to "sharpen the saw" in each of four dimensions.

Reflection is a key component of improving your teaching. After all, how can you possibly hope to fix gaps or problems if you don't take time to consider what went wrong in the first place? Without meaningful reflection, teachers are doomed to repeat the same failures over and over again. We encourage our students to be accountable for their mistakes and take steps to do better next time, and we should hold ourselves to the same standard.

ON WHAT I DID WRONG MS. B'S JOURNAL

Looking back at my first year teaching high school English, I can confidently say, I was pretty bad. Yep, you heard me. Stink, stank, stunk. I was lecturing way too much and asking the students all the wrong kinds of questions. Sure, I had my moments: inciting impassioned debates about ***Don Quixote*** *and facilitating a compelling research project on the Holocaust, among them, but for the most part, I was mediocre, at best. The one bright spot was that I was able to personally connect with students and feel deeply invested in their lives, but I knew I wasn't doing a good-enough job helping them connect to the material or, worse yet, helping them connect with each other. And it was heartbreaking. Here I was, so passionate about Shakespeare and* ***To Kill a Mockingbird*** *and even vocabulary, for Pete's sake, and I could not for the life of me see any of that passion, save for brief flickers, reflected back at me through the eyes of my students.*

What was I doing wrong? Is it too harsh to say "everything"? I left the classroom after that year and became a library media specialist, and then took a few years to stay at home with my own children, working as an education writer and consultant. As my youngest child prepares to begin her school journey, and I prepare to return to mine—a little wiser for the wear— I've come up with a to-do list for when I get back into a classroom.

1. **SHUT UP.** *No one wants to hear me talk. They want to explore, analyze, and create. They want to come up with their own ideas, not sit and listen to me blather on about my own.*

2. **Chuck the grading scale.** *This was a real thorn in my side, anyway, so good riddance. I hated assigning points, an exercise I never understood and always felt was completely arbitrary. Instead, I'll assign meaningful work and assess its completeness, or lack thereof, in a way that makes sense and promotes growth.*

3. **Give students autonomy.** *To me, nothing felt more strange about teaching than having to give almost full-grown human people permission to use the restroom. I mean, I understand the values of rules in the classroom, but this seemed like an overreach. In all the bathroom breaks I permitted, only one student went rogue, and, frankly, if I had to listen to me going on and on, I would've gone rogue, too. I'll take those odds. I want students to have autonomy over their learning and their bathroom breaks. My new tactic: have such an engaging classroom, the kids won't need to fake pee.*

4. **No more multiple choice.** *Ugh. I cringe at the multiple-choice tests I gave in my classes. I can now list a million and one fantastic, engaging ways to check for understanding, and there's nary a multiple-choice question among them.*

5. **Focus on learning, not teaching.** *I spent so much time that first year worried about what I was teaching, I didn't really think about what the students were learning. Even when I developed relationships with students and deeply cared for them, I still fell short facilitating their path to authentic learning.*

Does it feel good to look back and see how I failed my students in so many ways? Not really. But you know what? It's a heck of a lot better than refusing to look back at all. As teachers, reflection is a critical, nonnegotiable part of the territory. We have to constantly keep ourselves in check, because the stakes of our job are really high. Of course, I made mistakes my first year teaching, but I value myself and my students enough to reflect on those mistakes and figure out how not to repeat them. I think with a little time for reflection and willingness to admit past mistakes, any teacher can go from good (or, in my case, painfully mediocre) to great.

REFLECTING ON YOUR YEAR OF GROWTH

John Dewey, the renowned educational reformer, said, "We do not learn from experience, we learn from reflecting on experience." Now that you've spent a year entrenched in developing your growth mindset and fostering the growth mindsets of your students, it's time to think deeply about the process. What did you do well? What mistakes did you make along the way? Use this journaling guide as a way to engage in deep reflection about the process of creating a growth-oriented classroom.

Great teachers are engaging in reflective practice daily. Through reflection, a teacher can discover what worked in a lesson and what may need to be tweaked or thrown out altogether, or brainstorm ways to better engage a struggling student. Beyond daily reflection, however, it's also important to take a holistic look back on your practice at the end of the school year. We've developed this guided journal to help you conceptualize how growth mindset changed the way you teach and the way your students learn. To engage in this guided journaling exercise, answer some or all of these journaling questions and prompts. Don't just answer the questions! Take time to think about them, reread them, and use them for ideas on how to better use your mindset training in class next year.

Respond to some or all of the following questions and prompts.

Describe your mindset when you started this process.

____

____

____

____

____

____

Think of someone who has a growth mindset. What are they like? How do they approach life?

____

____

____

____

What were the initial barriers to implementing growth-mindset strategies in your classroom?

How would you describe your students' mindsets at the beginning of the year?

Describe how your students responded to learning about the mindsets.

Some of the questions my students had during our lessons were . . .

The ways I changed my classroom to reflect growth mindset were . . .

The ways I included parents in my growth-mindset journey were . . .

My favorite growth-mindset resources are . . .

Teaching my students about brain plasticity resulted in . . .

I incorporated brain development in my classrooms by . . .

Describe how your students responded to using metacognitive strategies.

Did using growth-mindset strategies improve any of your relationships at school?

Recall a time you encountered a person with a fixed mindset this year. How did you respond?

How did using growth-mindset strategies improve your relationship with parents?

This year, I challenged my students by . . .

Describe how you incorporate equity in your classroom practices.

Explain some key strategies you use to differentiate your instruction.

How can you improve on your differentiation practices?

I tried to incorporate my student's passions by . . .

How did you set and convey high expectations to your students?

Did learning about growth mindset change the way you praise your students?

Did learning about growth mindset change the way you offer feedback to your students?

How did your students engage in peer feedback?

I helped my students develop grit by . . .

How did goal setting help your students make improvements?

What are some efforts you made to normalize mistakes in your classroom?

Tell a story about how a mistake was turned into a learning opportunity this year.

My best strategy for coaching students through setbacks is . . .

A strategy I used to incorporate productive failure was . . .

Some ways I incorporated the principle of not yet were . . .

After reading the book, how did you change your approach to formative assessments?

After reading the book, how did you change your approach to summative assessments?

A "knowledge-able" task my students engaged in was . . .

Overall, how has growth mindset changed the way you teach?

How did your students' mindset change by the end of the year?

____

____

____

____

____

____

What difference do you think the growth-mindset training will make as your students advance through their educational journey?

____

____

____

____

____

____

Who has helped you along your growth-mindset journey? How did they help?

____

____

____

____

____

____

THE SUMMER HABITS OF HIGHLY EFFECTIVE TEACHERS

In the best-selling book *The Seven Habits of Highly Effective People*, Stephen Covey uses "sharpening the saw" as a euphemism for taking care of oneself. Covey lists sharpening the saw as one of his ubiquitous seven habits because he believes an essential part of achieving success in life is "preserving and protecting the greatest asset you have — you."[97]

Of course, that makes perfect sense, because, like our mantra for the month said, we can't take care of other people if we don't take care of ourselves first. But, let's face it, in the flurry of taking care of our students during the school year, our own needs often take a backseat. It would be great if we could be sharpening our saws all year long, but teachers spend much of the year in "giving" mode: giving their time, money, love, and attention to all the people who count on them, and finding themselves fresh out of saw sharpeners at the end of each day. This is why it's so important to spend time sharpening the saw over the summer. Covey says that there are four areas in which our saws need to be sharpened: physical, social/emotional, mental, and spiritual.

"Feeling good doesn't just happen. You can't just snap your fingers and decide to feel good without making a conscious effort," writes Covey. "Living a life in balance means taking the necessary time to renew yourself. It's all up to you."[98]

What better time than summer for teachers to enjoy the relaxation and renewal they've earned after a hard year's work? But treating yourself well shouldn't just happen in the summertime. Use this opportunity to develop positive self-care habits that can serve your mind, body, and soul year round.

A well-rounded self-care and preservation routine, no matter how small the effort, is essential to your holistic well-being and success. This summer, while time is on your side, seek to discover healthy self-care habits. You may have less time for them when school begins again, but you should always seek to find ways to incorporate feeling good and living a balanced life into your daily routine.

THE PHYSICAL DIMENSION

Teaching is physically taxing work. Teachers are in a constant state of motion — walking around the classroom, crouching down to talk to students, and running down the hallways. The job is far from sedentary. When teachers feel mentally tired and physically exhausted at the end of the day, they may forgo additional exercise. But we know that exercise has valuable benefits for the mind and body. Exercise is a proven mood booster that has the potential to increase energy levels, promote better sleep, improve overall health, and be fun. Yes, that's right: exercise can be fun!

We can sharpen our saws physically by incorporating exercise and healthy foods into our diets and getting the required amount of sleep. Did you know that the recommended amount of sleep for an adult is seven to nine hours? That kind of sleep may seem like nothing more than a dream during the school year, but summer is your chance to create positive sleep habits. Below are some suggestions for ways to incorporate exercise, healthy eating, and sleep into your summertime routine:

Go on a walk (or run). Buy a FitBit or other pedometer and try to get in ten thousand steps a day over the summer through running or walking. This is great exercise that doesn't require any gym memberships or special equipment. Consider exploring the thousands of awesome podcasts available online, and it'll be like exercise and entertainment rolled into one.

Do yoga. Yoga is an excellent restorative exercise. It clears your mind and challenges your body. Almost anyone can do yoga in a way that is safe and effective, and you don't even need a class! There are hundreds of yoga videos and tutorials available for free on YouTube. Roll out your mat and get posing.

Plant a garden. Gardening is a one-two punch of exercise and healthy eating. If you've ever pulled weeds, you know it's hard work. Planting a garden is a surefire way to incorporate exercise and healthy eating in your summertime routine. The exercise will come from tending the garden, and the healthy food will come from the fruits (and vegetables) of your labor.

Sleep in. Go to bed early, sleep in late, and take naps this summer, because you probably have some catching up to do. Sleep plays a critical role in health and well-being, and during the school year it often comes at a premium. So take time during the summer months to do a little hibernating. And, hey, if you decide not to take off your pajamas the entire day, that's okay, too.

Take a dance class. Or a kickboxing class, or a spin class, or a tai chi class — it doesn't matter, just get out there and get moving! Swimming is another beneficial exercise to engage in during the summer months. Teachers rarely have the opportunity to be the student, and taking an exercise class is a great way to get physical and put yourself in the student role at the same time.

THE SOCIAL/EMOTIONAL DIMENSION

Taking care of your emotional health is just as important as taking care of your physical health. It would be easy (and desirable) to shut your door and not leave the house for three months, but that probably won't serve you well in the long run. Engaging in social and emotional renewal means connecting with interesting people, engaging in practices that promote emotional well-being, and strengthening friendships and relationships that are often put on the back burner during the school year. Here are some suggestions for summertime sharpening of the social/emotional saw.

Join a book club. Or whatever kind of club you're into. Chess, weight lifting, stamp collecting, the *kind* of club doesn't matter. What matters is that you're spending time engaging in a subject that you're passionate about alongside people who share your interest.

Volunteer. Volunteering is a great way to feed your soul. Your community has many opportunities for you to get involved and volunteer. You may want to explore an opportunity that involves children, but also consider spending some time helping adults, animals, or the environment to experience something a little different from your typical day-to-day work with kids.

Meet friends for coffee. Or meet them for wine. Just take time over the summer to schedule regular dates with your favorite people. There's just something about belly laughing through dinner with a friend that makes you feel so good.

Get therapy. Talk therapy, art therapy, retail therapy, massage therapy — no matter what kind of therapy you subscribe to, engaging in some form or another is a great way to relieve tension and improve your mood.

THE MENTAL DIMENSION

We know, we know—you spent all year focusing on mental pursuits, and it's time to take a break! But here's the thing: you probably shouldn't take a break from sharpening your mental saw. You can, however, spend time exploring new ideas and opening your mind to new pursuits both in and out of the realm of teaching and education.

Take a class. Learn something new and enjoy being the student for once. Being a student may even open your eyes to new ways of teaching.

Read. Reading is a great way to learn, grow, and relax at the same time. You know that ever-expanding list of books you want to read but never have time for? Summer break is the perfect time to tackle it!

Teach. Yep, that's right. Teaching is a great way to sharpen your mental saw, and you're already a pro at it! Consider teaching a session at a summer workshop or conference. Teachers have many summer opportunities to share their best classroom practices with colleagues and peers; take advantage of one!

Write in a gratitude journal. Take time to write! There's something about putting pen to paper (or fingers to keyboard) that helps us connect to our emotions. Write about your life, your experiences, your gratitude—whatever. Just write! Journaling is a proven mood booster and mental saw sharpener.

THE SPIRITUAL DIMENSION

The fourth dimension Covey describes is the spiritual dimension. When you feel at peace with yourself, it's easier to reflect on your values, beliefs, and feelings in an authentic way. Whether you choose to pray, meditate, or otherwise reflect, it's important to engage in the intentional practice of calming yourself and looking inward. It's amazing what just ten minutes of quiet, focused reflection will do for your mind and spirit.

Get outside. There is something transcendent, almost therapeutic, about being in nature. Quietly enjoying nature nourishes our spiritual side like few other things can. Maybe it's the lack of gadgets, or, perhaps, the lack of people, but either way, taking time to enjoy the great outdoors is good for the soul.

Meditate. For many, meditation is a deeply spiritual experience. If you've never meditated, check out a book or instructional video on the topic. You'll learn to be still, relax your body, focus your breathing, let your mind drift, and soothe your soul from the inside out.

Attend a service. For many, spirituality is honed through religious practice. Try attending a service at a local church, mosque, synagogue, etc. You might even consider mixing it up to gain a new perspective.

Make art. Making art or music can be a deeply spiritual experience. The solitary act of making gives us time and space to focus on our task at hand, but also to examine our inner motivations and desires.

***

Sharpening the saw is all about taking care of yourself. You may have your own strategies for taking care of your mental, physical, emotional, and spiritual well-being, and that's great. Do whatever it is that helps you increase your energy, motivation, and mood. At the end of the year, teachers can often feel burned out, so finding ways to renew your spirit is essential to returning to school next fall ready to put your best foot forward.

12

JULY: A NEW DAY IS A NEW OPPORTUNITY TO GROW

You're off to great places! Today is your day!
Your mountain is waiting! So...get on your way!

—Dr. Seuss

OBJECTIVES

- ✓ Learn tactics for confronting fixed mindsets and getting the most out of learning opportunities.
- ✓ Develop an online personal learning network.
- ✓ Seek out growth-mindset resources to support you on your journey.

SHIFTING INTO LEARNING MODE

Most teachers don't really take summer off. They are busy developing curriculum, attending meetings, teaching summer school, or retooling their lessons. Sure, we hear from misguided people all the time telling us how good we've got it with our three months of vacation, but great teachers don't go three hours, let alone three months, without thinking about how they can improve. Many teachers shift out of teaching mode the last day of school and directly into learning mode — gobbling up the books they didn't have time to read during the school year, enrolling in continuing education and professional development classes, attending conferences and camps, and earning additional certifications, all while enduring those snide remarks from jealous nonteachers who like to take every opportunity to remind us just how easy we've got it. Taking time during the summer to relax and renew is an important practice for teachers, but so is engaging in learning opportunities often given short shrift during the hectic school year.

As you continue on your mindset journey, the intentional practice and cultivation of growth mindset should be included in your summer enrichment itinerary. You can learn more about mindset research by seeking out resources (hint: there are many listed at the end of this chapter!) to help develop your growth mindset and give you strategies for continuing to foster growth mindset in your students. In addition to formal learning on the mindsets, every day you get the opportunity to develop and hone your growth mindset by using it to confront situations in nearly every aspect of your lives.

Dweck writes in *Mindset* that every day presents us with opportunities to grow and help others grow,[99] and suggests developing a plan for seizing these growth opportunities when they present themselves.[100] She lists five situations in which people with growth-mindset tendencies find chances to grow and change and people with fixed-mindset tendencies will avoid at all costs. These five areas are challenges, obstacles, effort, criticism, and success of others.[101] Spend some time thinking about how you can approach these situations with a growth mindset, and seek out opportunities during the summer to practice.

Let's say that you're faced with tackling a tough professional development course over the summer. In the context of this course, you'll encounter the five situations

Dweck outlined. Let's take a look at these hypothetical situations and responses from both the fixed- and growth-mindset perspectives.

THE SITUATION	A FIXED MINDSET SAYS . . .	A GROWTH MINDSET SAYS . . .
CHALLENGE A day into the class, you realize it's going to be very challenging — more so than you anticipated.	"I'm outta here! I'll be in my comfort zone, if anyone needs me."	"It's worth a shot! The worst thing that could happen is I learn a little something."
OBSTACLE Uh-oh, the first assignment turns out to be a killer.	"I guess not everyone is meant to be good at this."	"Whoa! This was way tougher than I thought. I'm going to have to rearrange some things so I can devote more time to this."
EFFORT A big project requires familiarizing yourself with some new concepts and practicing new skills.	"I'm just going to do the stuff I know and work around the rest. No point into going to all that trouble for something that doesn't really matter."	"This is going to take a lot of work on my part, but if I can understand these skills and concepts, it's going to open a lot of doors for me in this area.
CRITICISM The teacher gives you some critical feedback on strategies you used to complete the project.	"I really don't value the teacher's opinion anyway. It was obvious she hated me the minute I walked in the door."	"The teacher makes some really good points on how I can improve this. I wonder if she'd be open to meeting with me to discuss more after class?"
SUCCESS OF OTHERS Tina got an A on her project, and you didn't.	"Of course, Tina got an A. But it wasn't an easy A; did you see how hard she had to work on her project? She's obviously not that smart."	"Wow! Tina's project was so well thought out and unique. I have got to pick her brain before the next project. She'll be a great resource to help me improve."

Approaching learning opportunities with a fixed mindset leads you down a path that all too often ends in frustration, jealousy, and throwing in the proverbial towel. But with a growth mindset, tackling something new and difficult is a chance to expand your horizons, meet new people, and gain knowledge. It's important to approach new learning challenges in the growth mindset so you can get the most out of them, but you also have an opportunity to help others stuck in the fixed mindset. Sometimes, all it takes is a little redirection.

A friend once told us about the time she was sitting through final student presentations as part of a college course. The presentations were the culmination of an entire semester's worth of research, and were clocking in at about fifteen minutes each. The class was ten presentations in with six left to go, and it was shaping up to be a long night—much longer than she'd planned for. The longer she sat listening to her classmates' presentations, the grumpier she became. Finally, she leaned over to the student next to her and complained, "I wish everyone would just hurry up so we can go home." Without taking her eyes off the presenter, the woman beside her whispered back, "But I'm learning so much! I especially learned a lot from yours."

Well, that put our friend in her place. She felt pretty embarrassed about her impatience and indifference to the learning opportunity before her. She regrouped, refocused her attitude and attention, and actually learned some new and interesting material that night. Sometimes the subtle rebuke of a fixed mindset is enough to send it packing. If someone around you is displaying a fixed mindset and missing a valuable learning opportunity, try reframing the situation in the context of the growth mindset. Let's take the previous example of the professional development class and respond to the fixed-mindset messages with a growth-mindset redirection.

A FIXED MINDSET SAYS . . .	A GROWTH MINDSET RESPONDS . . .
"I'm outta here! I'll be in my comfort zone, if anyone needs me."	"Don't leave! It's going to be tough, but we can do it together."
"I guess not everyone is meant to be good at this."	"I think if you stick this out, it'll be worth it in the end."
"I'm just going to do the stuff I know and work around the rest. No point into going to all that trouble for something that doesn't really matter."	"I think going to all that trouble is the point. The hard work is exactly what we need to get better at this."
"I really don't value the teacher's opinion anyway. It was obvious she hated me the minute I walked in the door."	"She's an expert at this stuff! If you think she doesn't like you, maybe you should talk to her personally?"
"Of course, Tina got an A. But it wasn't an easy A; did you see how hard she had to work on her project? She's obviously not that smart."	"I admire how hard Tina worked. We should ask her to be in our group next time. I think we could really learn a lot from her!"

We often hear teachers refer to themselves as "lifelong learners." Standards and best practices in education are constantly changing, so flexibility and growth are highly valued traits. But the reality is that the teaching field, like any profession, also consists of many with fixed mindsets refusing to try new teaching practices, serving up the same lessons year after year, and grumbling about professional development opportunities. More than likely, you're going to run into a few of them. The good news is that you can be an agent for change. A strong growth mindset not only gives you the tools to attack new learning challenges without fear of failure or inadequacy, but also the ability to help others who may be struggling with change. Remember, fear of failure and insecurity are powerful feelings, and dealing with them is often what sends people spiraling into their fixed mindsets. Offer struggling colleagues an opportunity to view the situation through the lens of a growth mindset. It may be just the thing they need to turn a missed opportunity into a seized opportunity.

#GROWYOURPLN

Today's teachers don't have to settle for whatever one-size-fits-all professional development their district coordinators are serving up at the bi-monthly in-services. They can be the masters of their own learning thanks to the infinite resources available through their online personal learning networks. Your personal learning network (PLN) is the group of people with whom you have made connections and developed relationships for the purpose of sharing ideas, collaborating, and talking about your profession in a way that seeks to enrich and enliven one another.

"In-person professional development is very useful, though it is brief and easily forgotten when not reinforced," says Jordan Catapano, an English teacher at James B. Conant High School in Hoffman Estates, Illinois, and avid Twitter-for-education user. "Social media is the key to extending the learning. Teachers can connect with other teachers and presenters they met in-person and continue their relationships. Teachers can also find additional resources, materials, and conversations that relate to the professional development content."[102]

Developing an online presence can be a valuable asset for teachers who want to connect using social media platforms like Facebook and Twitter. Twitter, in particular, has exploded as a go-to resource for teachers interested in developing their PLN, sharing resources, and chatting with like-minded educators. Teachers with a growth mindset are keen to seek out new ideas, perspectives, and opinions, in order to continually develop their teaching repertoire. Catapano initially joined Twitter to show his students that it was just another pointless time waster, but once he saw the rich conversations and resource sharing happening among teachers on the platform, he was hooked.

"Twitter has helped me become a leader in my school," says Catapano. "Social media keeps me on the cutting edge of education philosophy and practice, and I take what I'm learning online and communicate it to my colleagues. Twitter has introduced me to new concepts or tools, including growth mindset, Google Classroom, standards-based grading, modern classroom environments, and social bookmarking. I don't think I would have heard about these without social media. Now I feel better equipped to implement these elements into my classroom and to help teach others about them, as well."[103]

Twitter, for the uninitiated, is a social media network on which users post messages that consist of 140 characters or less. Teachers have gravitated toward Twitter as a place to connect and share ideas, and often find one another through the use of hashtags. Hashtags identify a word as a searchable topic of discussion. For example, #engchat is a popular hashtag used among English teachers looking to connect. You can search online for a list of hashtags that teachers in your content area are using on Twitter. Once you sign up, there's a learning curve, which means you'll have to keep a growth mindset about you in order to navigate learning the ins and outs until you find your rhythm. When you see another user posting interesting ideas, articles, pictures, and so forth that catch your attention, you can "follow" them. Their posts are then added to an automatically generated stream or feed that you see when you log on to your account.

"When I have a question, I swivel my chair and ask another English teacher in my office," says Catapano. "But there's only a few teachers in my office, and what if they can't answer my question or give me what I need? Building a social media PLN gives teachers literally thousands of others they can 'swivel their chair' toward and learn from."[104]

Growth mindset, in particular, has a large following among teachers on Twitter. Just search #growthmindset, and you'll find plenty of teachers discussing using the principles of growth mindset in their classrooms. Whatever topic you're interested in, be it growth mindset or some other aspect of teaching or education, you're almost guaranteed to find people discussing it on social media. And if they aren't, you can start the conversation. Here are a few social media platforms to explore as you form your personal learning network. You may already be using some of these in a personal capacity, but consider adding them to your roster of professional resources in an effort to grow your PLN.

SOCIAL NETWORKS FOR TEACHERS	
TWITTER	Teachers can follow other educators, post Tweets of 140 characters or less, link to interesting articles, and engage in Twitter chats based on certain topics pertaining to education. To access, go to www.twitter.com.
FACEBOOK	Join Facebook groups to connect with other educators on a variety of topics. There are groups dedicated to different content areas, grade levels, and educational concepts like growth mindset. To access, go to www.facebook.com.
PINTEREST	Pinterest is a social networking platform on which users "pin" links to articles, websites, photos, and blogs. It is a visually driven social media platform that boasts a large number of teacher users. To access, go to www.pinterest.com.
GOOGLE+	Google+ is the social networking arm of Internet giant Google. Google+ has a devoted following among teachers, many of whom find it through their Google Apps for Education account. Teachers can also use Google Hangouts to connect through video as part of their Google+ experience. To access, go to www.plus.google.com.
YOUTUBE	YouTube is an excellent source for professional development. There are untold numbers of tips and tutorials for educational technology and teaching, along with teaching videos and vlogs, among many other resources. Integrate social networking by subscribing to channels and commenting to and connecting with teacher users. To access, go to www.youtube.com.

Growth mindset means believing that there's no end to learning and exploration. Teachers have never had more access to diverse perspectives and ideas than they do right now. This summer, make an effort to delve into social networking in a professional capacity with the aim of growing your personal learning network and opening your mind to new ideas.

GROW YOUR GROWTH MINDSET

If the idea of growth mindset has captivated you, we assure you that there are many more resources on the subject to absorb. This fascinating concept, pioneered by

Carol Dweck, has roots in motivation, neurology, and behavioral science. It can be applied to children and adults alike, and used in virtually every aspect of life. We would like to leave you with a list of our favorite mindset resources. These are the works that we consult daily, that have opened our eyes to a new way of being, along with active online communities that continually offer revelatory ideas and opinions on the topic of mindset.

BOOKS

Better by Mistake: The Unexpected Benefits of Being Wrong, by Alina Tugend

Brain Rules: 12 Principles for Surviving and Thriving at Work, Home, and School, by John Medina

Creating Innovators: The Making of Young People Who Will Change the World, by Tony Wagner

Creative Schools: The Grassroots Revolution That's Transforming Education, by Ken Robinson and Lou Aronica

Drive: The Surprising Truth about What Motivates Us, by Daniel H. Pink

The Gift of Failure: How the Best Parents Learn to Let Go So Their Children Can Succeed, by Jessica Lahey

Grit: The Power of Passion and Perseverance, by Angela Duckworth

How Children Succeed: Grit, Curiosity, and the Hidden Power of Character, by Paul Tough

How We Learn: The Surprising Truth about When, Where, and Why It Happens, by Benedict Carey

Mathematical Mindsets: Unleashing Students' Potential through Creative Math, Inspiring Messages, and Innovative Teaching, by Jo Boaler and Carol Dweck

Mindset: The New Psychology of Success, by Carol Dweck

Mindsets in the Classroom, by Mary Cay Ricci

Outliers: The Story of Success, by Malcolm Gladwell

Peak: Secrets from the New Science of Expertise, by Anders Ericsson and Robert Pool

The Power of Habit, by Charles Duhigg

The Seven Habits of Highly Effective People, by Stephen Covey

Smarter, Faster, Better: The Secrets of Being Productive in Life and Business, by Charles Duhigg

The Talent Code: Greatness Isn't Born. It's Grown. Here's How., by Daniel Coyle

Talent Is Overrated: What Really Separates World-Class Performers from Everybody Else, by Geoff Colvin

Thinking, Fast and Slow, by Daniel Kahneman

Why Students Don't Like School: A Cognitive Scientist Answers Questions about How the Mind Works and What It Means for the Classroom, by Daniel T. Willingham

Why We Do What We Do: Understanding Self-Motivation, by Edward Deci with Richard Flaste

TED TALKS AND VIDEOS

"Brain Science" (YouCubed.org)

"Grit: The Power of Passion and Perseverance" by Angela Duckworth (April 2013, TED Talks Education)

"The Power of Belief," by Eduardo Briceno (November 2012, TEDxManhattanBeach)

"The Power of Believing That You Can Improve," by Carol Dweck (November 2014, TEDxNorrkoping)

"You Can Learn Anything" (Khan Academy)

WEBSITES

Mindset Online — www.mindsetonline.com, Carol Dweck's website devoted to mindset

Mindset Works — www.mindsetworks.com, mindset training website founded by Carol Dweck and Lisa Blackwell

The Character Lab — www.characterlab.org, research lab founded by Angela Duckworth

Mindset Kit — www.mindsetkit.org, free online mindset lessons from PERTS

YouCubed — www.youcubed.org, Jo Boaler's website, featuring mathematical mindset research

The Mindset Scholars Network — mindsetscholarsnetwork.org, research-based mindset information

Mindshift — ww2.kqed.org/mindshift/, original reporting on mindset science and application

ARTICLES AND PAPERS

"Carol Dweck Revisits the 'Growth Mindset,'" (*Education Week*, May 7, 2016)

"Fluency without Fear: Research Evidence on the Best Ways to Learn Math Facts," by Jo Boaler (YouCubed.org)

"How Not to Talk to Your Kids," by Po Bronson (*New York Magazine*, August 3, 2007)

"Praise for Intelligence Can Undermine Children's Motivation and Performance," by Claudia M. Mueller and Carol S. Dweck (*Journal of Personality and Social Psychology*, 1998)

"The Secret to Raising Smart Kids," by Carol S. Dweck (*Scientific American*, January 1, 2015)

A FINAL THOUGHT

Thank you for traveling this mindset journey with us. We hope that you've learned strategies and absorbed ideas that will serve you, your students, and your school going forward. Our greatest hope is that you take time to share the science and principles of growth mindset with colleagues and peers. If teachers truly believe that every child has the power to grow and improve his or her talents, skills, and abilities through hard work and effort, and seek to cultivate that belief in their students, the roots of the growth mindset will grow deep. Through you, growth mindset can bolster our future leaders, helping them overcome obstacles and setbacks, and lighting a fire for learning and growth that will, in turn, continue to empower children for generations to come. To continue the conversation on growth mindset, please visit us online at www.thegrowthmindsetcoach.com.

ENDNOTES

1 Carol Dweck, *Mindset: The New Psychology of Success* (New York: Ballantine Books, 2006).

2 Ibid., 15–16.

3 Ibid., 16.

4 Ibid., 7–10, 12–14.

5 Ibid., 7.

6 M. B. Roberts, "Rudolph Ran and the World Went Wild," ESPN.com, accessed March 10, 2016, https://espn.go.com/sportscentury/features/00016444.html.

7 Rudy International, "Rudy: The True Story," 2003, http://www.rudyintl.com/truestory1.cfm.

8 Nina Totenberg, "Sotomayor Opens Up about Childhood, Marriage in 'Beloved World,'" NPR, January 12, 2013, http://www.npr.org/2013/01/12/167042458/sotomayor-opens-up-about-childhood-marriage-in-beloved-world.

9 American Institute for Physics, "Marie Curie: Her Story in Brief," accessed March 10, 2016, https://www.aip.org/history/exhibits/curie/brief/index.html.

10 Nobel Media, "Malala Yousafzai — Biographical," accessed May 3, 2016, https://www.nobelprize.org/nobel_prizes/peace/laureates/2014/yousafzai-bio.html.

11 Carol Dweck, *Mindset: The New Psychology of Success* (New York: Ballantine Books, 2006), 10.

12 Ibid., 157.

13 Ibid., 245.

14 David Paunesku et al., "Mind-Set Interventions Are a Scalable Intervention for Academic Underachievement," *Psychological Science Online First*, April 10, 2015, doi: 10.1177/0956797615571017.

15 Carol Dweck, "Carol Dweck Revisits 'Growth Mindset,'" *Education Week*, September 22, 2015.

16 US Department of Education, "My Favorite Teacher," YouTube video, 2:03, posted May 6, 2010, https://www.youtube.com/watch?v=py46EaAscOA.

17 Teach.org, "Chris Paul Talks about His Favorite Teacher," YouTube video, 0:31, posted February 2011, https://www.youtube.com/watch?v=rRLCdmorqWA.

18 Teach.org, "Secretary of Energy Steven Chu Talks about the Influence of His Physics Teacher," YouTube video, 1:03, posted September 15, 2010, https://www.youtube.com/watch?v=erzflNDVaQs.

19 Teach.org, "Julia Louis-Dreyfus Talks about Her High School Physics Teacher," YouTube video, 1:05, posted September 15, 2010, https://www.youtube.com/watch?v=LLHZK3Un9qY&index=5&list=PLFDAB966A469ACDCA.

20 Paunesku et al., "Mind-Set Interventions," 7.

21 Ibid., 2.

22 C. Good, J. Aronson, and M. Inzlicht, "Improving Adolescents' Standardized Test Performance: An Intervention to Reduce the Effects of Stereotype Threat," *Applied Developmental Psychology* 24 (2003): 645–62 (found on MindsetWorks.com).

23 J. Aronson, C. B. Fried, and C. Good, "Reducing the Effects of Stereotype Threat on African American College Students by Shaping Theories of Intelligence," *Journal of Experimental Social Psychology* 38 (2002): 113–25 (found on Mindsetworks.com).

24 Dweck, *Mindset*, 201.

25 Ibid., 173.

26 C. M. Karns, M. W. Dow, N. J. Neville, "Altered Cross-Modal Processing in the Primary Auditory Cortex of Congenitally Deaf Adults: A Visual-Somatosensory fMRI Study with a Double-Flash Illusion," *Journal of Neuroscience* 32, no. 28 (2012): 9626–38.

27 David Eagleman, *The Brain: The Story of You* (New York: Pantheon Books, 2015), 116.

28 Ferris Jabr, "Cache Cab: Taxi Drivers' Brains Grow to Navigate London's Streets," *Scientific American*, December 8, 2011.

29 Jo Boaler, "Unlocking Children's Math Potential: Five Research Results to Transform Math Learning," accessed February 19, 2016, YouCubed.org.

30 Ibid., 4.

31 C. S. Dweck, "Mind-sets and Equitable Education," *Principal Leadership* 10, no. 5 (2010): 26–29.

32 Ibid., 27.

33 Donna Wilson and Marcus Conyers, "The Boss of My Brain," *Educational Leadership* 72, no. 2 (2014), http://www.ascd.org/publications/educational-leadership/oct14/vol72/num02/%C2%A3The-Boss-of-My-Brain%C2%A3.aspx.

34 Eric Nagourney, "Surprise! Brain Likes Thrill of Unknown," *New York Times*, April 17, 2001, http://www.nytimes.com/2001/04/17/health/vital-signs-patterns-surprise-brain-likes-thrill-of-unknown.html.

35 Rita Pierson, "Every Kid Needs a Champion," video file, May 2013, https://www.ted.com/talks/rita_pierson_every_kid_needs_a_champion.

36 Jeffrey Liew, "Child Effortful Control, Teacher-Student Relationships, and Achievement in Academically At-risk Children: Additive and Interactive Effects," *Early Childhood Research Quarterly* 25, no. 1 (2010): 51–64, doi:10.1016/j.ecresq.2009.07.005.

37 Jan N. Hughes, "Further Support for the Developmental Significance of the Quality of the Teacher–Student Relationship," *Journal of School Psychology* 39, no. 4 (2001): 289–301, doi:10.1016/S0022-4405(01)00074-7.

38 Rita Pierson, "Every Kid Needs a Champion," video file, May 2013, https://www.ted.com/talks/rita_pierson_every_kid_needs_a_champion.

39 Daniel Berry, "Relationships and Learning: Lecturer Jacqueline Zeller's Research and Clinical Work Highlights the Role of Teacher-Child Relationships," May 29, 2008, https://www.gse.harvard.edu/news/uk/08/05/relationships-and-learning.

40 H. Gehlbach, M. E. Brinkworth, L. Hsu, A. King, J. McIntyre, and T. Rogers, "Creating Birds of Similar Feathers: Leveraging Similarity to Improve Teacher-Student Relationships and Academic Achievement," *Journal of Educational Psychology*, accessed March 2, 2016. http://scholar.harvard.edu/files/todd_rogers/files/creating_birds_0.pdf

41 Hunter Gehlbach, "When Teachers See Similarities with Students, Relationships and Grades Improve," *The Conversation*, May 27, 2015, http://theconversation.com/when-teachers-see-similarities-with-students-relationships-and-grades-improve-40797.

42 Matthew A. Kraft and Rodd Rogers, "The Underutilized Potential of Teacher-to-Parent Communication: Evidence from a Field Experiment," October 2014, https://scholar.harvard.edu/files/mkraft/files/kraft_rogers_teacher-parent_communication_hks_working_paper.pdf.

43 Ibid., 3.

44 Ibid., 2–4.

45 Ulrich Boser and Lindsay Rosenthal, "Do Schools Challenge Our Students? What Student Surveys Tell Us about the State of Education in the United States," Center for American Progress, July 10, 2012, https://www.americanprogress.org/issues/education/report/2012/07/10/11913/do-schools-challenge-our-students.

46 Carol Dweck, "Even Geniuses Work Hard," *Educational Leadership* 68, no. 1 (2010): 16–20.

47 Interaction Institute for Social Change | Artist: Angus Maguire, "Illustrating Equality vs Equity," January 13, 201648, http://interactioninstitute.org?illustrating-equality-vs-equity/.

48 Ken Robinson, *Creative Schools: The Grassroots Revolution That's Transforming Education*, (New York: Viking, 2015), 51.

49 TeachingChannel.org, "Carol Dweck on Personalized Learning," video file, https://www.teachingchannel.org/videos/personalized-student-learning-plans-edv#video-sidebar_tab_video-guide-tab.

50 Robert Rosenthal and Reed Lawson, "A Longitudinal Study of the Effects of Experimenter Bias on the Operant Learning of Laboratory Rats," *Journal of Psychiatric Research* 2, no. 2 (1964): 61–72, doi:10.1016/0022-3956(64)90003-2.

51 Katherine Ellison, "Being Honest about the Pygmalion Effect," *Discover Magazine*, December 2015, http://discovermagazine.com/2015/dec/14-great-expectations.

52 Ibid.

53 Robert Rosenthal, "Four Factors in the Mediation of Teacher Expectancy Effects," in *The Social Psychology of Education: Current Research and Theory*, edited by Monica J. Harris, Robert Rosenthal, and Robert S. Feldman (New York: Cambridge University Press, 1986), 91–114.

54 Po Bronson, "How Not to Talk to Your Kid: The Inverse Power of Praise," *New York Magazine*, August 3, 2007, http://nymag.com/news/features/27840.

55 C. S. Dweck, "Mind-sets and Equitable Education," *Principal Leadership* 10, no. 5 (2010): 26–29.

56 Jennifer Gonzales, "The Trouble with Amazing," *Cult of Pedagogy*, January 25, 2014, http://www.cultofpedagogy.com/the-trouble-with-amazing.

57 Elizabeth Gunderson et al., "Parent Praise to One- to Three-Year-Olds Predicts Children's Motivational Frameworks Five Years Later," *Child Development* 00, no. 0 (2013): 1–16, https://goldin-meadow-lab.uchicago.edu/sites/goldin-meadow-lab.uchicago.edu/files/uploads/PDFs/2013%20gunderson%20praise%20paper.pdf.

58 Anya Kamenetz, "The Difference between Praise and Feedback," KQED's *Mindshift*, March 28, 2014, http://ww2.kqed.org/mindshift/2014/03/28/the-difference-between-praise-and-feedback.

59 Aubrey Steinbrink, email message to author, April 11, 2016.

60 Ibid.

61 Malcolm Gladwell, *Outliers: The Story of Success* (New York: Little, Brown, 2008).

62 A. L. Duckworth, T. A. Kirby, E. Tsukayama, H. Berstein, and K. A. Ericsson, "Deliberate Practice Spells Success: Why Grittier Competitors Triumph at the National Spelling Bee," *Social Psychological and Personality Science* 2, no. 2 (2011): 174–81.

63 K. Anders Ericsson and Robert Pool, *Peak: Secrets from the New Science of Expertise* (New York: Houghton Mifflin Harcourt, 2016).

64 "How to Become Great at Just about Anything," Freakonomics podcast, April 2016.

65 Daniel Pink, *Drive: The Surprise Truth about What Motivates Us* (New York: Riverhead Books, 2009), 119–20.

66 Carol Dweck, *Self-Theories: Their Role in Motivation, Personality, and Development* (Philadelphia: Taylor & Francis Group, 2000), 18.

67 Ibid., 18–19.

68 Martin Maehr and Carol Midgley, "Enhancing Motivation: A Schoolwide Approach," *Educational Psychologist* 26, nos. 3–4 (1991): 409–15, http://www.unco.edu/cebs/psychology/kevinpugh/motivation_project/resources/maehr_midgley91.pdf.

69 Chris Watkins, quoted in Debra Viadero, "Studies Show Why Students Study Is as Important as What," *Education Week* (blog), August 16, 2010, http://blogs.edweek.org/edweek/inside-school-research/2010/08/studies_show_why_students_stud.html?qs=Studies_Show_Why_Students_Study_is_as_Important_as_What_.

70 Denis Brian, *Einstein: A Life* (New York: John Wiley & Sons, 1996), 18.

71 Michael Balter, "Why Einstein Was a Genius," *Science*, November 15, 2012, http://www.sciencemag.org/news/2012/11/why-einstein-was-genius.

72 Ibid.

73 J. K. Rowling, "The Fringe Benefits of Failure," May 2008, video file, https://www.ted.com/talks/jk_rowling_the_fringe_benefits_of_failure.

74 Leah Alcala, "My Favorite No: Learning from Mistakes," video file, https://www.teachingchannel.org/videos/class-warm-up-routine.

75 Lisa Blackwell, "Grading for Growth in a High-Stakes World," *Mindset Works*, January 23, 2012, http://community.mindsetworks.com/tips-on-grading-for-a-growth-mindset.

76 Manu Kapur et al., "Productive Failure in Mathematical Problem Solving," http://www.manukapur.com/wp40/wp-content/uploads/2015/05/CogSci08_PF_Kapur_etal.pdf.

77 Annie Murphy Paul, "Why Floundering Is Good," *Time*, April 25, 2012, http://ideas.time.com/2012/04/25/why-floundering-is-good.

78 Katrina Schwartz, "How 'Productive Failure' in Math Class Helps Make Lessons Stick," KQED's *Mindshift*, April 19, 2016, http://ww2.kqed.org/mindshift/2016/04/19/how-productive-failure-for-students-can-help-lessons-stick.

79 Manu Kapur, "Failure Can Be Productive for Teaching Children Maths," *The Conversation*, February 18, 2014, http://theconversation.com/failure-can-be-productive-for-teaching-children-maths-22418.

80 Carol Dweck, "The Power of Believing That You Can Improve," November 2014, video file, https://www.ted.com/talks/carol_dweck_the_power_of_believing_that_you_can_improve?language=en.

81 Cory Turner, "The Teacher Who Believes Math Equals Love," NPR, March 9, 2015, http://www.npr.org/sections/ed/2015/03/09/376596585/the-teacher-who-believes-math-equals-love.

82 Sarah Carter, "Students Speak Out about A/B/Not Yet," *Math = Love*, June 17, 2015, http://mathequalslove.blogspot.com/2015/06/students-speak-out-about-abnot-yet.html.

83 Shelley Sopha, email message to author, May 3, 2016.

84 Ibid.

85 Ibid.

86 Ibid.

87 Michael Wesch, "Anti-Teaching: Confronting the Crisis of Significance," *Education Canada*, 48, no. 2 (2010), ISSN 0013-1253, http://www.cea-ace.ca/sites/cea-ace.ca/files/EdCan-2008-v48-n2-Wesch.pdf.

88 Michael Wesch, "From Knowledgable to Knowledge-able: Learning in New Media Environments," *Academic Commons*, January 7, 2009, http://www.academiccommons.org/2014/09/09/from-knowledgable-to-knowledge-able-learning-in-new-media-environments.

89 Buck Institute for Education, "What Is Project Based Learning (PBL)?, accessed April 21, 2016, " http://bie.org/about/what_pbl.

90 Ibid.

91 Andrew Kasprisin, "Our Transition to Standards-Based Grading," *JumpRope*, January 23, 2015, https://www.jumpro.pe/blog/our-transition-to-standards-based-grading.

92 Ibid.

93 "Two Wolves," accessed April 28, 2016, http://www.firstpeople.us/FP-Html-Legends/TwoWolves-Cherokee.html.

94 Carol Dweck, "Recognizing and Overcoming False Growth Mindset," *Edutopia*, January 11, 2016, http://www.edutopia.org/blog/recognizing-overcoming-false-growth-mindset-carol-dweck.

95 Dweck, *Mindset*, 244–46.

96 Dweck, "Carol Dweck Revisits 'Growth Mindset.'"

97 Stephen R. Covey, *The Seven Habits of Highly Effective People: Restoring The Character Ethic* (New York: Free Press, 2004).

98 Ibid., 131.

99 Dweck, *Mindset*, 244.

100 Ibid., 245.

101 Ibid.

102 Jordan Catapano, email message to the author, May 11, 2016

103 Ibid.

104 Ibid.

INDEX

D

E

F

H

I

J

K

L

M

N

O

P

R

S

T

V

W

Y

Z

ACKNOWLEDGMENTS

Thank you, first, to Carol Dweck, and her many colleagues, whose work inspired and informed *The Growth Mindset Coach*. Your groundbreaking revelations have changed the way I teach, learn, and live, and I am grateful for the work you have so generously shared with the world.

Thank you to my colleague, mentor, and friend, Heather Hundley. I am in awe of your passion for and dedication to the field of education. Your energy, optimism, and unwavering commitment to doing what is best for your students is something to be admired. I am so very grateful you took on the challenge of writing this book with me.

My appreciation to Shelley Sopha for sharing your insights. You are an exemplary teacher and amazing friend. Thank you to Aubrey Steinbrink (mrssteinbrink6.wordpress.com) for sharing your growth-mindset journey with me. Thanks to Sarah Carter (mathequalslove.blogspot.com) and Jordan Catapano (@BuffEnglish) for sharing your experiences. I am so grateful for teachers like you who take time to share their ideas and stories online so that we may all benefit from them.

Thank you to my parents, Gary and Cindy Moulin, and my parents-in-law, Clint and Kelly Brock, for the love, encouragement, and support you have provided. You were always ready to step in and pick up the slack when I needed to research or write. Knowing my children were well cared for while I worked on this book was an incredible gift. I am so grateful for all that you do.

As it turns out, it takes a village to write a book. Thank you to the wonderful people who provided support along the way: Jacob Moulin, Stevie Amos, Sam Moulin, Stephanie Switzky, Inga Nordstrom-Kelly, Amy Oldehoeft, Dr. Clint Colberg, Evelyn Colhouer, and Dalton Colhouer.

Thank you to the team at Ulysses Press for the opportunity to write this book. Special thanks to Casie Vogel, who provided support, encouragement, and guidance throughout the process, and to Paula Dragosh for her incredible attention to detail in editing this book.

Thank you to my children, Bodhi and Lila, who encourage and inspire me every day. To you, I say, "I really liked the effort you made to help mommy while she wrote this book." I love you both more than words can say. And, always, to Jared — my husband, my best friend, my number one fan. Thank you for believing in me, loving me, and supporting me even when it isn't easy. You mean the world to me.

Finally, Heather and I would like to thank the readers of this book. Teachers, your influence on this world knows no limit. You have the power to encourage curiosity, inspire discovery, ignite passion, and touch lives. We are all better off because of great teachers who work tirelessly to build a better tomorrow one, student at a time.

—Annie Brock

First and foremost, I want to extend a heartfelt thank you to Annie Brock for inviting me on this book-writing journey with her. She is an incredibly passionate writer and equally invested in empowering our youth to write the story of their lives.

I am eternally grateful for the opportunity to have worked with amazing students, educators, administrators, and professors throughout my career. These people (too many to name) have had a tremendous impact on my life.

Thank you to my parents, Roy and Carolyn Schlodder, who instilled in me the importance of hard work and encouraged me to always reach for the stars. I am grateful to my mother-in-law and father-in-law, Robert and Sharon Hundley, who have spent countless hours helping out while I was in classes or working on the book. To my children, Abbigail, Addison, and Abbott, thank you for your patience and grace as I continue to learn and grow as a mom.

And finally, thank you to my loving husband, Matt, for always believing in me, for your patience, your words of wisdom, the countless number of hours you have spent editing papers and the book, and for the encouragement to embrace new challenges. You make me a better person each day.

—Heather Hundley

ABOUT THE AUTHORS

Annie Brock is a former library media specialist and high school language arts teacher. She graduated with a degree in journalism and mass communications from Kansas State University and earned her teaching credentials through Washburn University. She currently works as a freelance writer and educational technology consultant. Annie previously authored *Introduction to Google Classroom*. She lives in Holton, Kansas, with her husband, Jared, and their two children.

Heather Hundley is an elementary educator with 12 years of teaching experience. She currently works as an Instructional Support Specialist with Greenbush Southeast Kansas Education Service Center. Heather has an elementary education degree from Washburn University and master's degrees in education and in school leadership from Baker University. She has served as a supervisor for pre-service teachers and as a guest lecturer at Washburn University. Heather was recently named a Kansas finalist for the 2016 Presidential Awards for Excellence in Mathematics and Science Teaching. She lives in Holton, Kansas, with her husband, Matt, and their three children.

Made in the USA
Columbia, SC
09 April 2025

3268b39c-eeee-447c-abf0-ba433ee3cfc7R01